AN UPWARD PATH

OF A DISCIPLE

A JOURNEY THROUGH
THE PSALMS OF ASCENT

Dr. Michael Lewis

Edited by

CHARITY LEWIS

with

KENNESAW MOUNTAIN TRAIL GUIDE

by JASON SCHMALTZ

An Upward Path of a Disciple

A Journey Through the Psalms of Ascent

Copyright 2020, Dr. Michael Lewis

ISBN: 978-1-7330412-0-1

Unless otherwise noted, all scripture is taken from the Holman Christian Standard Bible.

Maps were created with CalTopo and reproduced with permission. Special thanks also to Open Street Map contributors

Published by
Engedi Publishing LLC

Foreword

"...let us run with endurance the race set before us..."
HEBREWS 12:1

"...the way is narrow that leads to life."
MATTHEW 7:14

**How would you describe the "race" that we are each
to run in our journey of Christ-likeness?**

**How might you describe the challenges and possibilities of
living on the "narrow way" as a faithful disciple of Jesus?**

With personal vulnerability and insightful Biblical reflections , Pastor Lewis shares an inspiring portrayal of the "narrow way" that a faithful follower travels. Using the historical backdrop of the Jewish people's frequent and prayerful journey "upward" to Jerusalem and the Temple Mount, this captivating work gives definition to the "race" set before each of us that we might live as aliens and strangers in this world as we journey toward our New Jerusalem.

As with any journey , faithful pilgrims will be challenged to fix their eyes on the destination and in our case, Pastor Lewis challenges us in this well-written resource that our destination is the Person of JESUS!

Each Chapter equips us for the journey, being reminded that God has not left us without a "road map " but rather has given us the secure promise of success through living out His Word. As an excellent resource for small groups and one-on-one or discipleship triads , we are equipped to make this journey into Christ-likeness through faithful engagement with other followers of Jesus.

Allow His Spirit to lead you through this resource into frequent encounters with JESUS and His Word as you make this journey of Christ-likeness with fellow disciples.

Dr. David Ferguson
Executive Director
GreatCommandment.net

Dedication

"My heart is filled with gratitude for Charity Lewis' contribution in serving as the lead editor for this book. Charity is the oldest of our three daughters, and her gifts and talents in writing were used by the Lord to complete this project; without her, this book would not be possible. Charity devoted many hours and days sifting through sermon manuscripts and listening to sermons which I preached from these chapters of the Psalms of Ascent. It is a special joy in my heart as a father to experience joint accomplishment with Charity with the humble desire to serve others well. Charity is currently serving as Living History Interpreter at the Museum of the Bible in Washington D.C., and she is a graduate of the King's College in NYC. "

Special thanks to Jason Schmaltz for writing the Trail Guide experientials. It is a joy to disciple Jason and now see him making disciples who are making disciples. Jason is the husband of Anna and father of three precious children, Johnny, Naomi, and Heidi. Not only is he successful as an hydro-chemical engineer but he is also a strong passionate spiritual leader serving in the deacon ministry of Roswell Street Baptist Church and implementing the Summit Seekers ministry which is multiplying men to be disciples of Jesus.

AN UPWARD PATH
OF A DISCIPLE

Table of Contents

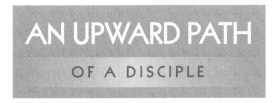

Preface

What are the Psalms of Ascent?

The Psalms of Ascent were prayers sung by God's redeemed people on their travels up to Jerusalem (Deuteronomy 16:16). The Psalms of Ascent are recorded in the Book of Psalms, which are contained in chapters 120 to 134. They are characterized by a sense of cheerfulness and hope. These fifteen psalms were likely sung in sequence by Hebrew pilgrims as they went up to Jerusalem to the great worship festivals.

Topographically, Jerusalem was the highest place in Palestine. Those who traveled to Jerusalem spent much of their time hiking. The ascent was not only a literal endeavor but also a metaphorical one: The trip to Jerusalem parallels a life of moving upward to God, an existence that advanced from one level to another in developing maturity. The apostle Paul described this as "the goal, where God is beckoning us onward - to Jesus" (Philippians 3:14, The Message).

I want you to use your imagination as you engage and lean into the Word of God: you are traveling together with the Hebrews, who would be your family and friends, to celebrate one of the three high and holy festivals of the year. As we would tread up the hills, we would hear a shofar and there would be shouts in the camp. There would be joy and laughter upon our lips because we are traveling upward. Every step that we take, our lives are moving upward in anticipation and worship unto the Lord.

What relationship does the Psalms of Ascent have for the follower of Jesus today in the New Covenant? The follower of Jesus is one of the redeemed people of God on a caravan pilgrimage upward to a high and holy city that is not the earthly Jerusalem, but the heavenly one, where we will enjoy the Marriage Supper of the Lamb for eternity. This path is upward and forward, never to be downward or backward. As the disciples travel upward together, the challenges require support and faith in the Lord to overcome the new heights that are reached. These new heights give the disciples clarity of sight and sounds. The journey is one of joyful songs filled with hope and anticipation of greater things yet to come.

As the body of Christ, we grow together, as there are many dangers outside of us. As we travel, we notice the elevation getting higher and we are able to see the landscape with a grander view than we have ever experienced before. This upward journey begins to deafen our ears to the chaos below and heighten our ears to the voice of God. The reward of hearing God's voice and seeing the results of long obedience is well worth the journey, although the journey is extensive and requires discipline. Many days and weeks are spent going upward to the festivals, and so it is for us as Christ-followers on this upward journey. There is nothing instantaneous about being a follower of Jesus; it is a process of growth and sanctification in our life. At the end of this pathway, there is a feast waiting for us. As the Israelites would celebrate The Passover, The Feast of Tabernacles and Jubilee, we are going to the great Marriage Supper of The Lamb; we are going to the celebration of the feast of our salvation as we travel together.

One can always enjoy the view of the mountain from below. However, God invites us into something grander and deeper than simply viewing His greatness from below. Spiritually, He desires for us to be climbers and not simply viewers of His grander purpose. In order to do this, pilgrims cannot endeavor to take the journey without taking their first steps.

Where do you want to be in your relationship with God? Where do you want to be in your relationship with others? If you want to be everything that God desires for you, start with the Great Commandment (Matthew

22:35-40). Secondly, obey the Great Commission (Matthew 28:18-20). From the Great Commandment and the Great Commission, Jesus outlines his vision and desires for our lives. A disciple is a learner, but not in the academic setting of a classroom; rather it is on a pathway of real-life walk with the living Lord Jesus. To be His Disciple says that we are people who spend our lives apprenticed to our Master, Jesus Christ. We are in a growing-learning relationship with Jesus.

A New Beginning

At some point, you may have witnessed at least one person whose life shows evidence that she or he has been with Jesus. You may have wished you could experience Jesus in the same way this person experiences Him, but don't know where to begin. Or you may sense there is an obstacle, visible or invisible, that gets in the way of knowing God fully.

Maybe you have experienced Jesus at one time in your life, or you used to be excitedly tuned into hearing His voice. In spite of where you may find yourself, let's take this spiritual journey together to the top. Jesus not only offers a new beginning, but he offers a new life. He wants to know you intimately; He longs to have a deep friendship with you. For someone to have a new beginning, something has to change.

As we journey through each chapter of the Psalms of Ascent, we will observe how the Spirit of God sets forth upward steps for us to take as disciples of Jesus today. The mission of Roswell Street Baptist Church is to make disciples of Jesus who "Love God, Love People, and Lead others to do the same." Imagine a world where disciples of Jesus make disciples who make disciples. Discipleship is God's ultimate upstream solution to the downstream problems in the church and culture. Let's walk together in the heavenly sunlight of God's Word on this upward path.

AN UPWARD PATH

OF A DISCIPLE

CHAPTER 1

The Beginning Step Upward is REPENTANCE

PSALM 120

1 *"In my distress I called to the Lord,*
and He answered me.
2 *"Lord, deliver me from lying lips*
and a deceitful tongue."
3 *What will He give you,*
and what will He do to you,
you deceitful tongue?
4 *A warrior's sharp arrows*
with burning charcoal!
5 *What misery that I have stayed in Meshech,*
that I have lived among the tents of Kedar!
6 *I have lived too long*
with those who hate peace.
7 *I am for peace; but when I speak,*
they are for war."

The First Step in the New Direction

One of my favorite weekly activities is hiking the Kennesaw Mountain National Park Trails as well as the trails located behind my home off of Cheatham Hill road, hiking the connection of paths up to Little Kennesaw Mountain and the top of Kennesaw Mountain. One thing I have learned is that in order to make a trip up the mountain, there are things I have to leave behind. I have to leave behind a desire to be a couch potato that sits in front of the TV and watches sports. I have to leave behind a preference for maintaining comfort. I have to set aside a schedule that is full, with emails and calls that require my attention. In other words, I have to give up a normal day of activities. So it is spiritually; if you are to travel the upward path of a disciple, you must leave certain desires and habits behind.

The very first command Jesus gave on earth is to repent (Mark 1:15), which is the act of turning from your selfishness and turning towards the Lord. John the Baptist preached on repentance in preparation for Jesus' coming: "Repent, because the kingdom of heaven has come near!" (Matthew 3:2). The early church called the hearers to repentance in Acts 3:19, "Therefore repent and turn back, so that your sins may be wiped out, that seasons of refreshing may come from the presence of the Lord." In order for new things to begin, old things have to be placed behind us. God calls us to repentance because it is the only way we will truly have a new beginning. Repentance is a change of mind that leads to a change of heart that leads to a change of life. Repentance, in military terms, is "an about face," a 180-degree turn in the opposite direction.

Turn From Lies

"In my distress I called to the Lord and He answered me."
PSALM 120:1

In verse 1, The Psalmist is praying for deliverance. "In my distress" means suffering and pain. Lies and deceit cause distress; they lead to pain or suffering in one's life that affect one physically, spiritually, emotionally, and relationally, leading to a desperate need. When you are in desperate need or in the midst of a stressful season, do what David did and call your troubles out to the Lord. I would also encourage you to not only jot down your prayers, but to jot down *specific* prayers. The Psalmist prayed specifically for God to deliver him from "lying lips and a deceitful tongue."

"LORD, deliver me from LYING LIPS and a DECEITFUL TONGUE..."
PSALM 120:2

Lying lips and deceitful tongues claim to be telling the truth, but they are falsehoods and distortions of truth. Have you been a recipient of a deceitful tongue? How does it feel when someone lies to you? It leaves you feeling betrayed and hurt. Maybe you have been deceived by a salesperson, a person of authority, a politician, or someone close to you.

Deceit always leads to distress. Maybe you are living in distress because someone who pretended to speak truth to you was telling a lie. Notice in Psalm 120:3 that the Psalmist experiences the pain of deception, in essence asking God, "God, what will you do to the betrayer?"

Slander and deception are serious matters, for they are of the devil. It is an act so severe that God will judge not only the devil but every person who has ever had a slanderous tongue and remains unrepentant.

"What misery that I HAVE STAYED IN MESHECH, That I have LIVED AMONG THE TENTS OF KEDAR!"
PSALM 120:5

What does it mean to live in Kedar and in Meshech? Meshech is a people group who lived far to the north of Palestine. Spiritually, Kedar was known to the Israelites as a far-away place and home to the second son of Ishmael. The Kedar people were a nomadic people of the desert. In this Psalm, Kedar represents a place of wandering that is going nowhere.

The Psalmist is saying that when you are wandering away from God, it is misery. Spiritually speaking, are you living in Kedar? Are you wandering through a maze of confusion where there is no real direction in your life? You may be wandering far away from God and from the relationships He has designed for your life. God's desire is that you become close to Him and that you live a life of purpose.

"I have lived too long with those who HATE PEACE.
I am for peace; but when I speak, they are FOR WAR."
PSALM 120:6

Maybe I'm talking to a student in school that would say, "Even in my school, I am living in a world that hates peace." Or maybe you're a businessman who dreads working with those who hate peace. Do you ever get tired of the conflict, hate, and constant fighting in this world? As a disciple of Jesus, there is always a growing dissatisfaction with the lies of this world and a longing for peace and truth. It raises a discontent for the way things are. Thank the Lord we are only passing through this world. Disciples are pilgrims and not wanderers of this world. Being pilgrims tells us that we are people who spend our lives going to God; we realize that this world is not our home and we set out for the Father's house.

If you love this world too much, you are miserable or are destined for misery. You will be in the place of Kedar, wandering from one place to another with no end. The only place that will bring anyone contentment is heaven, where fulfillment is found. Since life is a journey with two directions that we must choose from, consider the lies you must turn from and take the detour towards the truth.

Turn from Lies about God, Yourself, and Those Around You

The devil will never tell you the truth. The devil will pretend to tell you the truth but lead you into deceit (2 Corinthians 4:4). Satan is the father of lies, a slanderer. Satan's schemes aim to blind our minds from the truth about God and the Gospel. For instance, lies about God may have you believing He is distant, disappointed with you, or too busy to care. We sadly sometimes believe lies about ourselves, that somehow our life is an accident, we are not meant to be here, we have no purpose, or that we don't matter to other people. In Psalm 139 the Lord says otherwise: you were woven by God in the womb and He is acquainted with all your ways! You are His workmanship. Believe the Creator and not the creation.

Turn from the lies of those around you. Maybe the lies you believe about yourself could come from an unhealthy parent, advertisers, entertainers, psychologists, moralists, or false prophets. Turn from the lies of the advertisers who claim to know what you need, the lies of the entertainers who promise a cheap way to joy, and the lies of psychologists who offer to shape your behavior so you can live a long happy life. There are so many who "smile so sweetly and yet lie through their teeth" (Psalm 120:1-2, The Message).

Perhaps the biggest challenge of repentance is turning from the lies inside of us. The spirit within us wars against the flesh. There is a battle that is inside of us that is against God's Word. It is important to know the truth about your heart: it is deceitful (Jeremiah 17:9). If you follow your heart, it will lead you down, never up. Realize your flesh will seek to dominate your thinking and your spiritual life (Galatians 5:17).

How can we overcome the lies within ourselves? Speak truth as David did to Goliath in 1 Samuel 17. All David had in his hand was a sling and a stone. When Goliath showed off his sword, shield, bronze armor, and giant stature, David stepped out in faith shouting, "I come against you in the name of Yahweh of Hosts" (1 Samuel 17:45-51). The giant was touting out lies and deception about David. Have there have been taunting Goliaths telling you that you can't do great things for God, that you won't matter much, that you can't do much better in your life to fix your family or amount to anything? Yet what did David do? He turned from the lies and he ran with the truth. If you will walk forward by simple faith in God's truth, God will bring the victory.

Turn to the Truth

If you begin that upward climb, you must leave your comfort, turn away from lies, and turn to the truth. To say "no" to the comfortable lies will hurt temporarily, yet result in our long-term well-being in a way that brings gratitude for the "no's" in our lives. You will go from having holes to being made whole. Repentance is illustrated in the parable of the prodigal son in Luke 15. Every step he took away from the far country was a step of repentance into the Father's arms. He turned away from the world that first lured him and came home to the truth.

How often should we repent? Repentance is not an emotion or even feeling sorry for your sins; it is a decision. We must repent daily. It is deciding you have been wrong about believing lies and decide that Jesus Christ is telling you the truth.

If we notice, the Prodigal son didn't remain in his state of remorse for his sins and its consequences. He took the necessary steps of repentance, which meant traveling back home and facing what he thought would be humiliation from his father. He took a risk and counted the cost of embarrassment and the possibility of being a servant for the rest of his life. One must plan to take steps of repentance, whether it's a change of habit, removing bad company that may cause you to sin, or sincerely listening to God's voice about a call you have delayed to obey. Plan to take steps of repentance like forgiving the person who hurt you, loving your family unconditionally, reaching out to the new neighbor, or sharing the gospel with that co-worker or classmate that you keep putting off and saying "later." Repentance is an action. For the enemy, the action of obedience is a threat to his plan to steal, kill, and destroy your joy, since repentance is no longer an idea in the dark but a flaming light of sacrifice– a city set on a hill that cannot be hidden. Will repentance remain an idea or will it be put into action? Without repentance, no one will have victory over deceit but will live a life full of delusion.

How do I know what is deceit?

Notice that two times in Psalm 120:1-2, the Psalmist mentions "The LORD." The eternal, self-existent, all-knowing God desires a relationship with you and me. He is the truth and anything apart from Him is a lie. In a controversial world full of many gods, He says, "I am the way, the truth, and the life" (John 14:6).

We need to turn to the truth of Jesus. God the Father said, "This is my Son, the Chosen One; *listen to Him*!" (Luke 9:35). Listening to Jesus means that every day we need to encounter Jesus afresh. After all, you can't know someone without spending time with him/her. How much more is it with Jesus! When we encounter Jesus often, there is transformation that happens in our lives.

Sadly for many Christians, their *first* encounter of Jesus was their *last* encounter with Him. All the while, the living Jesus wants a relationship with you. He wants to encounter you in a new and fresh way. The last chapter in the New Testament, Revelation 22, says He is the Alpha and the Omega, He is the first and the last, He is the beginning and the end. Jesus is saying, "I Am" *above* the calendar and time, "I Am" the one who began your faith journey and ends your faith journey.

When experiencing fresh encounters with Jesus, usually early in the mornings, it is a time in which everything else and everyone else is tuned out and I am able to hear God more clearly. I am changed by Him, whether or not I wanted change. By spending time with God every day in his Word and in prayer, we can follow the truth and forsake the lies. We turn to the truth of Jesus found in the Bible. Here is the truth about you:

- God made you
- God loves you.
- God made other individuals.
- God loves them.
- Each person is therefore my neighbor.
- God rules and provides for the world.[1]

Turn to the Truth of the Bible

Are you facing a business decision? Open the Bible. Are high school seniors deciding where to go to college? Go to the Bible. Having problems in marriage? Open the Bible. The Bible is not a book full of holes; it is a *holy* book. All Scripture is God-breathed (2 Timothy 3:16). Here are two challenges I have for you:

- Read through the entire Bible for one year.
- Read the word of God daily.

Without the truth of God's Word, how would one expect to know the difference between truth and falsehood? How can we live a life that is set apart for God without consistently looking at examples of Jesus and the people of faith who have come before us?

Turn to the Truth of Fellowship

Proverbs 13:20 reminds us that *"the one who walks with the wise will become wise, but a companion of fools will suffer harm."* And as simply stated in the New Testament, *"Bad company corrupts good morals"* (1 Corinthians 15:33).

In our world full of lies, it is encouraging to have a place where we meet with those called the people of God. You may ask, "How often should I come to church?" Come as often as you can; seek for 52 Sundays in a row to worship with the people of God. If you are not able to attend a local church, you can livestream worship or visit a church where you are traveling. If you are not involved in a small group, get into a small group. All believers need the fellowship of God's people. To be delivered from "deceitful tongues" we must be surrounded with those who speak truth.

It is hard to leave the comfort of lies and apathy, but we must get out of the valley and go through an ascent that gets you into real climbing. As it starts to get more difficult, you've got to be extremely cautious. In the upward ascent, you are increasingly fatigued and wonder if you are going to make it. At this point, you've got to determine if you will push yourself to the top or come back down. The next part is climbing to the top and seeing the full picture; this is when you feel like a victor! Based on Psalm 120, I want us as the body of Christ to endeavor on a spiritual journey to knowing God deeper while being changed by Jesus. This begins with repentance.

Repentance is like making a U-Turn when driving an automobile. Have you ever driven on the road or highway following your navigation system and you begin to daydream, only to realize you missed your exit? I have found that in Atlanta, there are only two types of people on Interstate 285- the quick and the dead. The other day I was driving while thinking about something and cruised past my exit. Now what did I do when I passed the exit? Did I keep on going? Of course I didn't. I found the next exit to make a U-turn so that I could go back in the right direction. That's what God is calling us to do today. He is calling us to make a U-turn from the wrong way, from the lies of this world and the deception of this world, and He's calling us to follow after the truth.

If you have never trusted Jesus and you desire to enter this relationship with Him, today is the day of salvation! For those who are believers in Jesus Christ, this day is also the day of repentance. Maybe you used to be in a closer relationship with Jesus than you are today. You may say, "I used to be spiritually on fire for Jesus; I used to be so excited, I used to be passionate about the Word of God and about my church," but somehow, you have drifted. In Revelation 2, Jesus is speaking to the church of Ephesus saying, "You have abandoned the love you had at first." What Jesus is saying is that, although you have left Him, your first love, it is time for you to return to Him.

Upward Discipleship Challenge:

- Pray Psalm 120 several times, realizing that this Psalm is to be prayed from your heart and not admired at a distance. Pray for the Lord to deliver you from all deceit around and within you.

- Go upward by reading God's Word daily. Locate on YouVersion from your phone, tablet or computer at **http://bit.ly/2iGsjkh**.

- Make a goal of attending a small group and plan to worship as often as possible with the church. If traveling, visit a church or worship online.

- Read Psalm 121 in preparation for the next chapter.

AN UPWARD PATH
OF A DISCIPLE

CHAPTER 2

Where Are Your Eyes Focused?

PSALM 121:1-8

¹ *I lift my eyes toward the mountains.*
Where will my help come from?
² *My help comes from the Lord,*
the Maker of heaven and earth.
³ *He will not allow your foot to slip;*
your Protector will not slumber.
⁴ *Indeed, the Protector of Israel*
does not slumber or sleep.
⁵ *The Lord protects you;*
the Lord is a shelter right by your side.
⁶ *The sun will not strike you by day*
or the moon by night.
⁷ *The Lord will protect you from all harm;*
He will protect your life.
⁸ *The Lord will protect your coming and going*
both now and forever.

Where are your eyes? It is very important that we have the right focus. What we find on this climb of ascent requires focus. We are to seek the kingdom of God first, yet often we find ourselves looking down. For instance, consider the use of looking down at our smart phones "all the time." According to the *Cross Platform Future in Focus Report*, the average American adult (18+) spends 2 hours and 51 minutes on their smartphone every day. That is nearly 86 hours a month![2]

There is an historical and architectural significance to steeples. In early America, steeples were constructed so that our eyes would look upward. Just as little children look up to their parents leading them upward on the path, so must we have a childlike dependency on God as He leads us through our temporary homeland on earth.

As we look at this Psalm, it corrects numerous misunderstandings of what it means to follow God upwards. Most disciples don't make it past this understanding; sometimes believers mistakenly think that committing their lives to Jesus means that they will not have problems. There will be no more diseases, there will always be money in your bank account, you will always get along with your spouse, and that your children will grow up to be angels. What one can examine in Psalm 121 is that the life of a disciple is not the absence of difficulties but is the presence of God in the midst of our difficulties. Psalm 121:1-2 presents the Lord as the Creator of the heavens and the earth. Verses 3-4 say He is the Lord that never sleeps or slumbers. Verses 5-7 say that He watches over us day and night. Verses 7-8 tell us that He protects us from evil. His wonderful attributes show we can count on Him for strength.

"Where will my help come from?
My help comes from the Lord, the Maker of heaven and earth."
PSALM 121:1-2

As the Psalmist appears to be talking to himself in verses 1-2, it reveals how much humans engage in self-talk in our own minds. Even now you are talking to yourself in response to this book, to this Psalm, or maybe you are thinking about the next meal and not paying attention (as I do sometimes)! Nevertheless, what we say to ourselves is very important. We all practice "self-talk" and we must learn to practice healthy self-talk from the Word of God.

The word *help* means to give assistance or support. At the top right corner of a computer screen, there is a *help tab*. One may ask where the help tab is in life. When we don't know where to turn or don't know what decision to make, where or to whom do we turn?

The Psalmist says, "I will lift up my eyes." In other words, I will lift up my desire, my aspirations, my expectations to God. One can imagine the Old Testament people of God singing this Psalm in a caravan journeying up the hills to Jerusalem. On those hills, they cautioned themselves for bandits and robbers. They had to beware of any potential danger surrounding them. When you look to the hills, there may be anxiety filling in your heart, but as you see the hills getting steeper, it builds up anticipation of coming closer to the feast and worship of our God.

That being said, when you are on a journey, travelers must have awareness. If you are in the sun for too long, you can get a sunstroke. Some say the moonlight can cause epileptic seizures. It is said that people can become emotionally faint by what the ancients called a *moon stroke*. Possibly, these high places on the hilltops in ancient times refer to the location of pagan shrines, where the gods were believed to have lived. If one feared the sun's heat, he would go to the "sun priest" and pay for protection from the "sun god." If one was fearful of the malign influence of the moonlight, she would go to the moon priestess and buy an amulet. If one was haunted by a demon who could use any pebble under one's foot and trip the traveler, that person would go to a shrine and learn a magic formula to ward off mischief. These are the actions that some would take in order to protect them from harm. In this Psalm, the Psalmist answers his own question, *"My help comes from the Lord who makes the heavens and the earth."*

I have a pastor friend in Asheville, North Carolina, who says that there are all types of people who go up to the mountains in his hometown of Asheville for more than the view alone. Some of them go with the goal to grasp a control and feeling of nature with a new strength and new replenishment– it's what we call Zen-Buddhism or New Ageism. If individuals confuse a love for nature in this manner, as if creation would help them rather than the Creator, it is no different than seeking the gods of Asherah and Baal. Ideas such as Pantheism or Buddhism are like the gods who offer false hope, for they have *"eyes, but cannot see; ears, but cannot hear; hands, but cannot handle; feet, but cannot move"* (Psalm 115:6). The mountains have no inherent strength in them. In the context of the Near Eastern religions during the time of the Psalmist, he indicates how his help is not from the gods but from Yahweh (Psalm 121:2). Looking up to the hills for help will always end in disappointment. It will leave you futile, empty, restless, and uncertain. Climbing to the top would have no meaning if it is all defined by subjective reasoning rather than objective truth.

We look not to the mountains but to the majesty of the Maker of the mountains, the Creator of the heavens and the earth. Believers have a different worldview than those who do not know Jesus. The word of man is always changing, but God's Word never changes. It is infinite; it is eternal. After God spoke, everything came into being (Genesis 1-3). He is able to be our helper. He has more than enough strength to help you.

"Indeed, the Protector of Israel does not slumber or sleep."
PSALM 121:4

Notice in this Psalm, the Lord never goes to sleep. I remember when I was eighteen years of age as a young pastor, I was invited by my professor from college to travel with him and preach the Gospel in India. I had hardly been out of the state of Georgia or South Carolina and here I am getting on an airplane! I will never forget that as I was preaching to 400 pastors who gathered to hear the Word, a Hindu priest began to crank up a strange sound, yet I continued to preach over it. Later I asked my professor about the loud noises and clanging. He explained that it was the sound used to wake up their Hindu gods. At that moment I realized the significance of Psalm 121:4. Out of the numerous false gods, Yahweh is our helper, our

Creator, and our Sustainer who never needs to be awakened.

May I ask you where you are looking for your strength? Don't look out in the world, because you will be disappointed. Don't look inward, lest you get depressed. Don't look below you where there is darkness, but look up to the Lord. Open up His Word every day and listen to His voice. If you can, put two knees on the floor and pray. It is important that we have this childlike focus daily so we can be strengthened.

Remember the account in the Gospel when Jesus walked on water, but the disciples were scared that He was a ghost? When the disciples began to recognize Him and Jesus called out to Peter, Peter began his first steps on the water looking towards Jesus. One can imagine the awe and wonder of this moment for Peter. As a Jew, he had heard how God opened the Red Sea for his ancestors in deliverance from Egypt and now he is walking on the water by the power of the Messiah. However, once Peter looked around at the storm, distracted by the dangers of the wind and the sea, he sunk and nearly drowned.

This encounter with Jesus is a great reminder of what our life is like as Christ followers. If we have our eyes on Jesus, we can do the supernatural by His strength. We can have the strength to live the Christian life victoriously. We will have the strength to overcome the luring temptations in our lives. We can have the strength to enjoy healthy marriages, families and friendships. But when our eyes are off of Jesus, we begin to sink.

Notice in verse 3, the Psalmist says that the Lord will not allow your foot to slip. When you are walking through life as well as the path up Kennesaw Mountain, there are many obstacles - rocks, roots, and uneven surfaces. If a hiker were to trip over any of these obstacles, he or she risks injury for weeks. So it is in life. There's a tendency for us to slip and stumble.

A mentor once told me, "All of the water in the ocean cannot sink a ship unless it gets in it. And all of the evil of the world cannot bring a person down unless it gets in one's heart." The Lord will not permit evil to overtake you. Stability comes from these attributes and provisions from God:

1. His Presence

2. His Promises

3. His Provision

Anyone can appreciate the Gospel and say "Amen" on Sunday, but what about on a Monday? Or on a Wednesday? We may look to the advice of celebrities, of unwise friends or co-workers for advice on how they deal with certain issues. A believer can very easily try to make-do without being mindful of the promises of God. On an average daily routine, it is hard even for God's people to be mindful of Genesis 1, that there is an omniscient, omnipresent God who is watchful of every step you take. He will not allow your foot to be moved. He desires to give you stability. There is not one place, not one problem, not one peril that you will face by yourself. God has promised He will be with us.

> *"The Lord protects you; the Lord is a shelter right by your side.*
> *The sun will not strike you by day or the moon by night."*
> **PSALM 121:5-6**

Notice in verse 5 that one of the things that the Lord protects us from are storms. When people were traveling in ancient times (including the people of Israel), they would have to take cover in a cave or other location for shelter. The Lord promises He will be our Shelter. Another danger the Lord protects us from are sunstrokes– the sun will not strike you by day from the loss of sanity; the moon will not strike you by night. He will deliver you from all evil, from all distress, and from harm. That's security.

What is the call of God? It is to turn our eyes to Jesus. Look to Him for help. Look to Him for strength (Hebrews 12). Why would anyone want to look elsewhere?

> *"The next step upward is childlike focus."*
> **PSALM 121**

Madison is a young girl who is a member of our faith family. As Madison would look up to her mother and father as her guide on the hiking trail, so should we depend on God to guide us in our earthly journey to our eternal destination. At six years old, nearly all of us depended on a parent/guardian. As children, we may have thrown a fit more often than we'd like to admit about ourselves. Little ones may react through temper tantrums because they either lack understanding or dread the discipline and momentary discomfort of boundaries; nevertheless, they depend on their parents for security. How much more should we continue to depend on God our Father, even when we don't understand His ways?

> *"The Lord will protect you from all harm; He will protect your life*
> *The Lord will protect your coming and going both now and*
> *forever."*
>
> **PSALM 121:7-8**

The word *security* rings true for many. In preparation for an unexpected crisis, many forms of security are set in place, such as insurance and retirement savings. From the time you begin your faith journey to the end of your earthly life, the word *protect* means the Lord will be your Protector. Notice that the Lord refers to himself as being our *Protector* six times in Psalm 127!

One of my favorite biographies is the life of David Livingston. A doctor from Britain, He departed from England for Africa in 1840, and became one of the greatest missionaries who brought the Gospel to certain tribes in Africa, where the Gospel continues to spread today through his influence. Before he stepped on the ship for Africa, he prayed Psalm 121, knowing his help came from the Lord. The dangers of traveling by sea prompted Livingston to pray for protection.

The Bible happens to depict God's people pleading for help on many hills. On Mount Moriah, Abraham was about to sacrifice his son Isaac until God provided a ram. On Mount Sinai, Moses brought down the law of God that is written today on our hearts as Christ followers. On the Mount of Calvary, Jesus died on the cross. On the Mount of Olives, Jesus ascended into heaven. It was on a mountain where the Spirit carried John the Revelator, where he experienced God's revelation, "I also saw the Holy

City, new Jerusalem, coming down out of heaven from God, prepared like a bride adorned for her husband. Then I heard a loud voice from the throne: 'Look! God's dwelling is with humanity, and He will live with them. They will be His people, and God Himself will be with them and will be their God. He will wipe away every tear from their eyes. Death will no longer exist; grief, crying, and pain will exist no longer.'"

It is as if God showed us his grand portrait from Genesis to Revelation, "Look beyond the hills for help, because I will be your Sufficient Provider." The ultimate redemption story is Jesus being our Protector and Rescuer.

God is not only mindful of your needs but He cares for you. If you are weak and weary, look to Him for strength. If you are struggling with problems or stumbling in sin, look to Him for stability. If you are fearful or uncertain, look to Him for security. In spite of how difficult our circumstances appear, God our Father is working in the lives of His children.

Upward Discipleship Challenge:

- Look up the Kennesaw Mountain Trail Guide on Page 121. Make a trip to the Boulder Areas on Little Kennesaw Trail and experience Psalm 121.

- Look up to the Lord by reading daily the Word of God. Based on your reading, what is one thing God is saying to you? Write your insights down and share with a friend.

- Commit to memory Psalm 121:1-2 and meditate on God's help for your life's struggles.

- Reflect on what it means to be a "pilgrim and stranger" in this world as a disciple of Jesus. How does this contrast to being a "settler" who conforms to this world? Discuss with a friend. Consider Hebrews 11:8-10, 13-16; 1 Peter 2:11.

CHAPTER 3

The Longing Step of the New Journey

PSALM 122

1 *I rejoiced with those who said to me,*
"Let us go to the house of the Lord!"
2 *Our feet are standing*
within your gates, O Jerusalem!
3 *Jerusalem—built as a city should be*
solidly joined together,
4 *where the tribes, Yahweh's tribes, go up,*
to give thanks to the name of Yahweh.
(This is an ordinance for Israel).
5 *There, thrones for judgment are placed,*
thrones of the house of David.
6 *Pray for the peace of Jerusalem:*
"May those who love you prosper;
7 *May there be peace be within your walls*
and security within your towers!"
8 *Because of my brothers and friends,*
I will say, "Peace be with you."
9 *Because of the house of the Lord our God,*
I will seek your good.

Jerusalem is a high and holy City in the Old Testament that not only holds historical significance for the people of Israel, but also has a place prophetically for all (Revelation 22). It is the place where salvation of the world was provided by God's Son. The Old Covenant was to the people of Israel what the New Covenant is to the believer today. For the follower of Jesus, the upward path is a longing step of worship. When believers look up instead of looking around, they long to worship the Lord with a heart of joy. David says, "I was glad when they said to me, let us go into the house of the LORD" (Psalm 122:1, New King James Version). David expresses a heart of joy, a heart of delight, not drudgery, but eagerness.

Longing to Worship the Lord with a Joyful Heart

"I rejoiced with those who said to me, 'Let us go to the house of the Lord'"
PSALM 122:1

As the pilgrims ascended into Jerusalem, they had a longing in their hearts to celebrate Passover in the spring, Pentecost in the summer, and the Feast of Tabernacles in the fall. On their way, they likely experienced anticipation, a longing in their hearts to stand in the courts of God, hear the Word of God and sing praises about Him. Psalm 122 is a description of what is to fill our hearts every day as followers of Jesus. We should have an individual longing to come into the presence of God. Is it not what many Christians feel when they gather together as the body of Jesus Christ and worship together?

In Atlanta, it is said that the price of tickets to the National Championship College Football game on the lower level can go up to $3,000! Imagine if someone offered a chauffeur to transport you to the front of the Mercedes-Benz Stadium and also reserved seats for you in the best seating zone of the game? What if this generous person also said you could invite all the friends and family you want? Would it not bring so much excitement and gratitude to your heart? How much more is the gift of God's grace that saves us from what we deserve and invites us to the best seating in His kingdom for worship?

In this Psalm, David is reflecting on the time when he was first invited by friends to worship and the joy which he experienced as a result of that invitation. Do you remember who first invited you to worship? Does gratitude come to your heart for their thoughtful invitation? Who are you inviting to join in worship and experience the presence of God? In cultural Christianity (in the state of Georgia for instance), it is easy to complain about menial issues, such as the lighting and the music, yet 92% of Cobb County does not attend church anywhere. People who don't know Jesus usually don't care if the church has the most upgraded building and technology. What most people are looking and longing for are meaningful relationships, the kind that can satisfy the greatest desire of their hearts, which is a relationship with God. In bringing ourselves and others to worship, here are factors that cause us to have joy as we worship the Lord: The presence of God, the Word of God and the people of God.

1) The Presence of God

> *"You reveal the path of life to me;*
> *in Your presence is abundant joy;*
> *in Your right hand are eternal pleasures."*
> **PSALM 16:11**

What is impressive is not the interior decoration of a church or the height of the steeple. The greatest thing about a church is the risen Jesus who is among us as we gather in His name. Our worship is not centered on a PLACE, but we are centered on the PERSON of our Lord Jesus Christ!

2) The Word of God

> *"Your words were found, and I ate them.*
> *Your words became a delight to me*
> *and the joy of my heart,*

for I am called by Your name,
Yahweh God of Hosts."
JEREMIAH 15:16

I oftentimes teach the Word of God with a smile on my face because I have so much joy in being filled with the Word of God. I am honored and thrilled to impart the Word of God to the church body. I do not seek to preach at people nor to people, but to sincerely minister His Word to hearts. Whether you hear the Word of God in a church body or read it at home, let the Word steep in your mind and heart like a tea bag steeping in hot water. The longer the tea bag steeps, the more flavor the tea will produce. Savor God's words as you would delicious food, beautiful music, or your favorite sports team. I hope we not only remain steepers of God's sweet words but share what was steeped within us to our neighbors and even our enemies.

3) The People of God

"Not staying away from our worship meetings, as some habitually
do, but encouraging each other, and all the more as you see the
day drawing near."
HEBREWS 10:25

I love the family of God at Roswell Street. It is a joy to see older members investing in the lives of the younger generation. In the 2017-2018 school year, our International Learning Center enrolled over 500 from more than 30 countries. Every week we are becoming more and more like heaven made up of every tribe, tongue and language as described in Revelation 7:9.

"Because of my brothers and friends, I will say, "Peace be
with you."
PSALM 122:8

It is beautiful how David refers to fellow believers as family. Let me encourage you to be a habit-maker of worship. Unless you are stricken with sickness or have a severe circumstance, please don't miss a day of worship. I visited a senior adult one day who told me that she watches my sermons on livestream every Sunday from her hospital bed. A tear began to fall from her eye as she expressed, "Oh Pastor, I wish I could be with you. I wish I could be with my church family."

If you were to ask believers from parts of the Middle East or a closed country like China and North Korea the question - "What would prevent you from gathering with God's people to worship?" - they would answer differently than what we would in the West. They would say, "If I die," or "If the church building was burned down." In China, four buildings were burned to the ground in January of 2018. One of my friends from China says that the average member drives two hours to his church because that is the closest location to meet with a body of fellow believers.

I'm sure many are busy this year, this month, and even this week. However, worship, like other weekly events, gives structure to life. There is structure in the knowledge that you will be at a certain place at a specific time with a specific group of people once a week. Have you ever experienced a day when you didn't feel like going to church, yet you went anyway and you came away refreshed, thankful that you worshipped? Worship, prayer, hearing the Word, and being encouraged while also being held accountable are a few among many blessings a believer can receive from their local church body.

Long to Worship the Lord with a Thankful Heart

"Jerusalem…where…Yahweh's tribes go up to give thanks to the name of Yahweh."

PSALM 122:3-4

David encompasses a sense of gratitude in Psalm 122. When we come to church, for what blessings that we have freely received can we give thanks to Yahweh? Psalm 103:1-2 says, "My soul, praise Yahweh, and all that is within me, praise His holy name. My soul, praise the LORD, and do not forget all His benefits."

We can rejoice in the Lord because He has been so merciful to us; He forgives us, He redeems us, He renews our strength like the eagle. We can give thanks to Yahweh for choosing us as adopted children in Christ and for sealing us with His Holy Spirit! We thank Him for forgiving us of our sin and for redeeming us out of sinful bondage (Ephesians 1:1-8). We can bless the Lord for all that he has done! When you come to worship the Lord, come with a grateful heart. Sometimes it is easy to forget the Lord's faithfulness and come into worship with a complaining heart instead of a thankful heart.

Long to Worship the Lord with a Prayerful Heart

"Pray for the peace..."

PSALM 122:6

I remember the first time I attended a midweek prayer gathering as a middle schooler. My dad invited me to come along with a small group of older men. I was frightened because I had the impression that prayer was said aloud with fanciful words that I could seldom understand. As the prayers began to flow from these men's hearts, it became clear that prayer was a transparent and sincere act from their hearts. I began to learn to pray by bowing my head in agreement with their prayers. What happened that evening instilled in me a desire to pray.

When you think about coming to church, do you think about praying? If someone begins praying in worship, a healthy habit of prayer will form and fulfill a person's longing for peace, which only comes from God. Notice in verse 6, it says to "Pray for peace." The original term for peace is *shalom*, which speaks about peace or well-being that results from God's will being completed in a person. My wife and I pray for our three young adult daughters and their future. When their wedding day comes, I'm certain tears will be rolling down my face and I will say to them, "I pray that you will have the richest blessings of God upon your life and marriage." Shalom is when you are holding a newborn baby in your arms and praying for God's complete will to be fulfilled in the baby's life. Shalom is seeking God's peace over our lives, our families, as well as our communities.

In the text, the Psalmist is praying for the Shalom of Jerusalem. Jeremiah 29:7 says to pray for the welfare of the city. Ninety-two percent of the people in my community of Marietta, Georgia do not attend church. It gives me a burden to pray for spiritual awakening to occur in our hearts so that God will do the same for them as He has done for me. As I drive through my neighborhood, I pray for the shalom of God to fill every home. My prayerful ambition for Roswell Street Church is to become a church where disciples of Jesus make disciples who "Love God, Love People, and Lead others to do the same."

The call of the body of Christ is to be faithful. One major but simple act of faithfulness is prayer and intercession, including our prayers of shalom over the Church. The Great Commandment of our Lord sums up the heart of worship, to "Love the Lord your God with all your heart, soul, mind and strength."

We can minister to God by showing up with a thankful heart. God ministers to us, but we have a chance to minister to Him, which is another way of worshipping Him. I admire the moments when my daughters come and thank me for something I have done for them; it ministers to my heart. If their thankfulness is significant to me as an earthly father, how much more does it mean to our heavenly Father?

Why do you love God? One compelling motivation as to why we love God is because He first loved us. Encounter Jesus and His love for you; picture Jesus hanging on the cross in your mind. Imagine the sign placed above Jesus' head has your name on it. Jesus died for you; He was taking your place in the death you deserved. Pause and respond with your heart to Jesus. Express your compassion for Him who died for you. Express your gratitude for His startling love. Express your love for Him. Now worship Him with a heart of joy, thanksgiving, and surrender!

Upward Discipleship Challenge:

- Practice worshiping the Lord by showing up in His Presence with a joyful, thankful and listening heart each morning.
- Invite friends to join you in worship this week with your local faith family.
- Commit to memory Psalm 122:1-2. Make this your confession of anticipation for public gather to worship the Lord.

CHAPTER 4

The Necessary Step of Ascent–
SERVICE

PSALM 123

¹ *I lift my eyes to You,*
the One enthroned in heaven.
² *Like a servant's eyes on his master's hand,*
like a servant girl's eyes on her mistress's hand,
so our eyes are on the Lord our God
until He shows us favor.
³ *Show us favor, Lord, show us favor,*
for we've had more than enough contempt.
⁴ *We've had more than enough*
scorn from the arrogant
and contempt from the proud.

Psalm 123 demonstrates a necessary step of service, a continuous call for all believers as Jesus himself demonstrates and testifies, "The Son of Man did not come to be served, but to serve and give His life—a ransom for many" (Matthew 20:28). It is true that we all serve something or someone. We can serve ideas, humane causes, corporate companies, selfish thoughts or sadly even Satan. Did you know that the condition of a servant is dependent on the character of his/her master? If you have a good master, you have a good quality of life. Think about this: Jesus is a wonderful Master because His love is unlimited. His grace gives us everything that we don't deserve, His provision is always sufficient and His power is able to meet every need.

The Psalmist sees himself as a servant of the Lord. A servant is someone who is employed or bound to serve and perform duties for another person. From slaves to highly esteemed positions of civil service, this term covers a wide range of social positions in the Biblical world. In both the Old Testament and New Testament, the title "servant of the Lord" is an important designation for key figures whom God uses to carry out his purposes.[3] Service is a willing, working, and doing in which a person acts not according to his own purposes or plans, but with a view to the purpose of another person and according to the need, disposition, and direction of others. [4]

A disciple is one who serves by loving the Lord, loving one another loving the church and being a loving witness. Because Jesus our Lord and Master washed the feet of His disciples, we are also to wash one another's feet. To clarify, it is not through good works of service that we are saved. One is not saved **by** "good works" but one is saved **to** "good works" (see Ephesians 2:9-10). Since we are saved, we are free to serve the one and only master who loves us unconditionally. The full strength and heart of service can only be grasped by experiencing God's love.

Serve By Loving The Lord

"I look to you, heaven-dwelling God, look up to you for help."
PSALM 123:1, THE MESSAGE

The psalmist's posture is looking up at God, not looking down, or to the right, or to the left. We can be blessed as we look to Him with anticipation, as "a servant's eyes on his master's hand." When the psalmist compares God to a *master*, God is not a master who is looking to catch you for doing the wrong task. In Isaiah 30:18, the text states, "The Lord is waiting to show you mercy, and is rising up to show you compassion." This is a God who looks upon you with excited grace - arms open, welcoming you.

> *"Like a servant's eyes on his master's hand,*
> *like a servant girl's eyes on her mistress's hand,*
> *so our eyes are on the Lord our God*
> *until He shows us favor."*
>
> PSALM 123:2

My family has a little dog named Debby who appears to be a snowball running around our house. Every morning, Debby knows I'm going to the pantry to pull out the wet dog food. She runs to me, stands on her two hind legs, and begs for food. Not only does Debbie depend on me for her meals, she also trusts me as her master. My reflection on this daily occurrence is a reminder that I do the same to God, looking with confident expectation of His provision for my life. Just as Debby looks to my hand to bless her, so the Lord longs for us to look to His hand because He wants to bless us. As my dog wants to please me and comes to me for attention, we can serve the Lord by giving Him our attention.

As a pastor who encourages our faith family to read the Bible and have a devoted time of prayer daily, the most common concern I receive from our members is not having enough time. If you are too busy to read God's Word, your life is much busier than the Lord intends. God created humankind in the first place so that they may love, know, and serve Him. By giving the Lord our attention, we as His

Debby

servants receive the blessing of His directing hand to appoint us to our work, His supplying hand to give us our portion in due season (Psalm 104:28),

His protecting hand to defend us when wronged, His correcting hand to redirect our behavior, and His rewarding hand to favor our obedience. 5

Begin lifting Your eyes to Him. Love the Lord by giving Him thanks such as, "You are merciful, even though I don't deserve mercy," or, "I praise you for being the Creator." Whatever you notice about the Lord, praise Him for it!

A sincere way to give the Lord attention is by yielding to His voice. Submit to Him as Jesus submitted to the Father. Obedience is not a step of blind faith. Rather, obedience is trusting an all-knowing God who reveals His will by His Spirit in His Word. Say yes, even before you know or understand what His good and perfect will is for you. As we submit all areas of our lives to the Lord, pray specific prayers. Prayer is a magnifying glass of what God is doing in ways we may not notice in the busyness of a day-to-day schedule. Write them down in a journal or a prayer list. As you pray, read God's Word daily and see what He reveals to you about Himself. He will answer you first and foremost through His Word and His Spirit. He may show you through opened and closed doors or the wisdom of godly people and circumstances. He has revealed Himself to believers in the 21st century through supernatural acts that many imagined happened in Biblical times only. Many Muslims have come to faith in Jesus by the appearance of Jesus in dreams and visions. Persecuted Christians have witnessed God's rescuing hand from dangers similar to Daniel's rescue from the Lion's Den. Whether by miracles, His word, or the Holy Spirit, we are to give the Lord our yieldedness to His voice and approach His voice with anticipation and faith.

> *Show us favor, Lord, show us favor,*
> *for we've had more than enough contempt.*
> *4 We've had more than enough scorn from the arrogant*
> *and contempt from the proud.*
> PSALM 123:3-4

The word *favor* holds equivalent meaning to the word *mercy*. The upward look to God in the heavens does not expect God to stay in the heavens but to come down, to enter into our condition, to accomplish the vast enterprise of redemption, and to fashion His eternal salvation.

We serve the Lord by anticipation and by faith. Psalm 123:3 implores, "Show us favor Lord, show us favor."

Do you have God's favor in your life? There is nothing else that matters more than the favor and loving kindness of God.

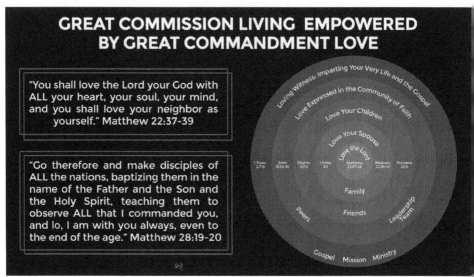

© *Great Commandment Ministries' Pastoral Care & Development*

Serve by Loving your Near Ones

"Serve one another through love. For the entire law is fulfilled
in one statement:
Love your neighbor as yourself."
GALATIANS 5:13-14

Let's consider and reflect on the diagram outlining concentric circles of relational care based on Jesus' teaching in the Great Commission and Great Commandment. Notice the center circle of the diagram. God is at the center of where we place our service and attention. The next circle centers on the "near ones: in our lives. The word neighbor means "near one." If you are married, your spouse is a priority as your "near one." Husbands are to sacrificially love their wives, and wives are to respect their husbands. If you have children or friends, they are your "near ones." Parents are called to love their children and children are called to love their parents. We are to "serve one another through love" (Galatians 5:13).

It sounds like an ideal concept, but how does one go about loving their "near ones?" Love is a lifestyle of giving first. Instead of prioritizing what you can receive during the course of the day, think about what you can give. We all have relational needs. Think about how you can meet the needs of your near ones. We all have needs of support, attention, affection, and appreciation. For instance, if your spouse washes the dishes, say thank you–show appreciation. If a family member faces a challenge, take the time to listen and show support. It can be as simple as carrying in the groceries from the car or sending an encouraging text. Maybe you can meet the need of approval, like telling your son or daughter, "I am so proud of you." Look for the relational needs of your near ones and take an opportunity to meet them:

- Need for approval – by saying "You did a great job"

- Need for attention – by saying "Tell me about your day"

- Need for appreciation – by saying "Thank you"

- Need for respect – by saying "I value your opinion" and then listening

- Need for security – by saying "I am here for you"

- Need for comfort – by saying "I hurt with you"

Serve By Love Expressed in the Church

In order to love one another as Christ loved us, it means we come with a servant-mentality over a consumer-mentality. Don't ask what the church can do for you; ask how you can bless those who make up the church. Church is a community with relationships, not a club of privileges.

I am thankful for one of my good friends, Mark Young, who oversees a group of volunteers whose task is to welcome and assist the first-time guests into our church. By mobilizing a welcome team, Mark and the volunteers are filling the needs of the church's first-time guests to feel welcomed. Church is more than the people who fill up a building or space; church is often filled with the names of people we know and have yet to know. How many people do you know by name? The only way we can really love our neighbor is to know our neighbor. I've observed people who go to church together all their lives, yet sadly, do not know one another. What if the church is known as a place where people are less alone because of caring relationships? Imagine if people always left church feeling less alone than when they previously came? The church is a place to serve God and serve others by meeting the needs of attention, support, and comfort. It is always encouraging to hear one of our faithful members say, "I don't know what I would do if it weren't for our church family."

Serve By a Being a Loving Witness

The most impactful way of sharing the Gospel is by serving others and sharing with others what the Lord has done for you. The message of the gospel is not pointing down to someone saying, "Come be like me. I'm better than you." It will take more than just giving a gospel tract; it's time to roll up our sleeves. A loving witness is a servant who has been saved and reconciled by the grace of God and who is now serving the Gospel to those around him. Paul says, "We were pleaed to share with you not only the gospel of God but we also our own lives" (1 Thessalonians 2:8).

It will take caring for people in meaningful ways. This means living every day as a missionary, whether it's on a middle school campus or in the workplace. Wherever you go, your life is sacred to God and you are to live your life as a missionary to the Lord.

Pause for a moment and reflect on the diagram of the concentric circles of relationships. With a spirit of young Samuel, pray "Speak, Lord, for your servant is listening" (I Samuel 3:10).

Which area of the concentric circles of relationships would the Lord have you give more attention to serve more effectively? Which area of your life would the Lord have you reprioritize? Maybe the Lord is overlooked in your attention. Maybe you haven't loved your spouse, your children, or your parents well. Maybe the Lord is placing a servant's heart in you to build up the body of believers. The Lord wants you to serve more effectively as a witness. As the Lord identifies that specific area of relationships, sincerely yield your heart to Him in surrender and ask Him to deepen your love in that area.

For those of you who are actively serving the Lord, I want to exhort you to be an ambassador for Christ, for Jesus said, "The Son of Man did not come to be served, but to serve, and to give His life—a ransom for many" (Mark 10:45). A ransom is a debt paid to release a captive. The only way we could be liberated from sin is payment through a ransom. That ransom was the death of Jesus on the cross, hanging as a compelling reminder of why we serve. God saved us so we could be free to serve Him and honor Him with our lives. Express gratitude to the Lord for His sacrifice.

Upward Discipleship Challenge:

- Read through the Kennesaw Trail Guide on Page 123. Visit the Illinois Monument Trail and experience Psalm 123 in that context.

- Discuss with a friend why the Bible teaches that we are "saved to serve" and not "saved by serving." Reflect on Ephesians 2:8-10.

- Draw out the Concentric Circles of Relationships on paper. Prayerfully ask the Lord to which relationship He would have you give greater attention. Join Jesus in loving others well.

- Reflect your present state of service in the church and community; ask the Lord where He would have you to serve.

- Talk to a leader of the area you feel led to serve this week. Pray through Psalm 123 with the view of Jesus as your Master.

CHAPTER 5

The Upward Path of Joy

PSALM 126

[1] *When the Lord restored the fortunes of Zion,*
we were like those who dream.
[2] *Our mouths were filled with laughter then,*
and our tongues with shouts of joy.
Then they said among the nations,
The Lord has done great things for them.
[3] *The Lord had done great things for us;*
we were joyful.
[4] *Restore our fortunes, Lord,*
like watercourses in the Negev.
[5] *Those who sow in tears*
will reap with shouts of joy.
[6] *Though one goes along weeping,*
carrying the bag of seed,
he will surely come back with shouts of joy,
carrying his sheaves.

When was the last time you were filled with joy? The Psalmist is reflecting on a time of *past* joy in verse 1. He also expresses a *hopeful* joy for what the Lord will do in the future. Notice the prayer of the Psalmist in verse 4, "Lord, restore our fortunes." Without Jesus, there is no inherent joy. 1 John 5:12 says, "The one who has the Son has life. The one who doesn't have the Son of God does not have life."

What is Joy?

First understand what joy is NOT. Joy is not money, pleasure, entertainment, or even doing good deeds. Joy is not doing what feels good, for the word "joy" conveys a trust that surpasses a fleeting feeling of happiness. Especially in an age of depression and anxiety, can someone have Jesus and not have joy?

According to Psalm 51, a believer can lose his or her joy as the Psalmist cries to the Lord, "Restore the joy of your salvation to me." If one's joy has been lost, where can one regain it? The Psalmist is filled with joy as he looks back at what God has done. Center your mind on the past aspect of what God has done and on the future aspect of what God will do in your life. Would your closest friends and family be able to tell that you have been with Jesus by your demeanor of joy? There is joy and celebration that comes with being a part of the people of God.

Find Joy by Appreciation

"When the Lord restored the fortunes of Zion, we were like those who dream."
PSALM 126:1

Discover joy as the Psalmist with appreciation. Reflect on a time where you last experienced joy and regain it by appreciating the Lord for what He has done. When the people of Zion lost their fortunes, the Psalmist is remembering how God restored them. God took evil and restored it to something good. Restoration happens in a conflictive marriage, when Jesus gets in the center of the couple. Restoration happens in the midst of broken family relationships, when Jesus enters and reconciles those who are opposed to one another.

One interpretation claims that this psalmist was celebrating Israel's deliverance from the oppressive toil of Egyptian slavery. The people of Israel lived in Egypt for 430 years, making bricks under the shadow and whip of Pharaoh, a life full of toil and anguish. Several centuries later, God brought deliverance through Moses. God took them from making bricks to marching through the Red Sea shouting these words, "I'm singing my heart out to God--what a victory! He pitched the horse and the rider into the sea. God is my strength, God is my song, and yes! God is my salvation!" (Exodus 15:1-2, The Message).Their spirit of awe compelled them to tell the world the wonders of the God whom they served.

Psalm 126:1 also reminds us of what David went through in the wilderness. He was hiding from King Saul, who sought to take David's life out of jealousy for God's favor on him. After several years of fleeing for his life, God gave David a song, recalling how the Lord restored to him the fortunes of Zion.

Historically, this Psalm has also been referred to those who returned from the Babylonian Captivity. The Babylonian exile was a dark time for Israel- rape in the streets, cannibalism in the kitchens, and captives forced to walk 600 miles across the desert in chains against the taunting mockeries of their captors. Jeremiah called the people to repentance, Isaiah preached a message of hope, and Hosea called the unfaithful people back to God. When Cyrus the Great of Persia conquers the Babylonians and signs a decree, the exiles were able to return home! The temple that was destroyed by the Babylonians was rebuilt in Jerusalem during the days of Ezra. This brought the people back to the city and they were singing Psalm 126, "When the Lord restored the fortunes to Zion." From one of these acts of God, the Psalmist prompts the people to celebrate and appreciate Him.

"Our mouths were filled with laughter then,
and our tongues with shouts of joy.
Then they said among the nations,
'The Lord has done great things for them.'"
PSALM 126:2

There are some matters in our lives that only God can control. It is in these times we humbly confess, "If God does not do it, nothing good will be accomplished."

In these times, we need restoration. The term *restore* means the reversing of a perilous situation to a prosperous situation (returning the situation to the way it was before calamity hit). The Psalmist views restoration as a great testimony among the nations. The nations would have heard them singing this psalm as the Israelites were returning from exile on the way to Mt. Zion. Joy is attained from giving thanks to God for what He has done.

Pause and consider: What Great things has the Lord done for You? It may be your salvation or the reconciliation of a broken relationship. Share with a friend or small group and rejoice together. I recall when the Lord restored me from a time when I was spiritually back-sliding in my teen years. My heart grew indifferent to the things of God, yet the Lord extended mercy by placing Godly people in my circle who encouraged me to abide in Christ. Buddy Hucks, a student minister from a small church in Richmond Hill, Georgia, influenced me to follow the Lord with my whole heart. It was a time of restoration that still fills me with a joyful appreciation.

Develop Joy by Anticipating the Great Things God Will Do

"Restore our fortunes, Lord, like watercourses in the Negev."
PSALM 126:4

The Psalmist is praying that God will continue to refresh and restore His people from captivity. He prays, "Bring back now your exiles." Notice that the Psalmist likens it unto "the water courses of the Negev." If you travel south of Judah, there is an arid place where the Dead Sea is located. In that area, there is a total barren desert– nothing lives there. Yet in the case of rain, the desert turns into torrents of rushing water, transforming this parched land into a beautiful garden, filling the land with a floral fragrance. Psalm 126:4 is a beautiful depiction of God's grace in our lives. Without Jesus, we are like a dead barren land. Through our Lord Jesus Christ, God has opened up the heavens; He has poured out living water into our hearts and that is what brings back His fragrance into our lives.

"Those who sow in tears will reap with shouts of joy.
Though one goes along weeping, carrying the bag of seed,
he will surely come back with shouts of joy, carrying his sheaves."
PSALM 126:5-6

Some sheaves of joy sprout from seeds of sadness and pain. Joy may not always begin with a smile etched on our faces; in fact, the Psalmist indicates that joy may begin in tears of mourning. For Israel, it was their captivity. For others, they may mourn the loss of a loved one, the loss of health, the loss of a job, the loss of a dream, or the loss of any hope. Plant that seed of mourning on good soil, which is on the truth of God's word filled with His promises. Take your sadness to God, trusting that He will answer you and restore you. Restoration is like planting a crop; it is a process of growth, transformation, and wholeness. The Lord can take a tragedy in your life and transform the seed into a fruitful crop of joy for the kingdom of God.

Jesus talks about being sowers of seeds and reaping the harvest. Jeremiah throws the seed out and asks the Lord to bring His people back from captivity. Ezekiel asks the Lord to raise the valley of dry bones back to life. Hosea begs God to return his adulterous wife as He does the people of God. As we go forth weeping and bearing precious seeds, be confident that God will bring it to fruition, as we doubtless will come again with bundles of wheat, rejoicing, into the high and holy city.

Is there a hope in your heart? Is there an anticipation? Some may have no hope due to living in sin. This God is mighty to lead us out of our sin into His joy as we anticipate what He will do beyond our past, taking us into abundant life.

Do you see Jesus as joyful? Or do you see a mistaken view of a disappointed or even distant Jesus with His back away from you? The latter picture is not the real Jesus of Scripture. The real Jesus has joy; He desires to give it to you so that you may be complete.

Upward Discipleship Challenge:

- Days 1–2: Reflect on *joy* as presented in Psalm 126. Write down the great things the Lord has done for you and give Him thanks. Write down the great things you anticipate the Lord to do for you and pray with faith for the future.

- Days 3–4: Pray Verses 4–6 for the future of the church. Ask the Lord to restore and revitalize His church through hearts empowered by His Spirit compelled to express His love.

- Days 5–6: Pray through Psalm 120-127. Meditate on the "Upward Steps" the Lord is calling you to as His disciple.

CHAPTER 6

The Upward Journey Involves Family

PSALM 127

[1] *Unless the Lord builds the house,*

its builders labor over it in vain.

Unless the Lord watches over a city,

the watchman stays alert in vain.

[2] *In vain that you get up early*

and stay up late,

working hard to have enough food—

yes, He gives sleep to the one He loves.

[3] *Sons are indeed a heritage from the Lord,*

children, a reward.

[4] *Like arrows in the hand of a warrior*

are the sons born in one's youth.

[5] *Happy is the man*

who has filled his quiver with them!

Such men will never be put to shame

when they speak with their enemies at the city gate.

THE UPWARD JOURNEY INVOLVES FAMILY

Psalm 127 is a song that was either composed by Solomon in relation to the construction of the first temple in Jerusalem or was composed by an exile in relation to the rebuilding of the temple. [6] Though most Psalms give praise to God or plea for His help, this Psalm of wisdom is intended to instruct people. Only when we allow the Lord to instruct us on building our relationships can we succeed.

The Construction of Relationships Requires the Lord's Blessings

If you are a disciple of Jesus and have a family, invite your family to go on this upward climb with you. By involving your family, you are following the great commandment, "Love the Lord your God with all your heart, with all your soul, with all your strength, and with all your mind; and your neighbor as yourself" (Luke 10:27).

Your neighbor is simply your *"near one."* If you are married, your spouse is considered your *near one.* If you have a parent, your parent is your near one. If you are a parent, it is imperative to lead your children upward. If parents are not leading their children upward, the world is more than happy to lead them downward. Hence God has set the role of fathers and mothers to demonstrate and instruct their children to love God (Deuteronomy 5:6). A thriving family doesn't develop on its own strength or magically pop out of nowhere; it must be cultivated by mom and dad.

It takes intentionality to be active and not passive in rearing children. As a father, it means I hold family devotions- this can look like your family gathering around the coffee table with the Bible and praying together. I always like to say that a family that prays together stays together. Prayer is timeless. Prayer not only brings you closer to the Father, but also brings you closer to your near ones.

Allow the love that you experience from God to be expressed in your daily encounters with people. In doing so, loneliness is removed from the lives of your near ones by creating togetherness within your marriage, family, and friendships. When the storms of this life come crashing at your doorstep, only a house built on the solid foundation of Jesus will stand. In the parable of the builders, Jesus makes a distinction between the wise man and the foolish man in the following passage.

*"Therefore, everyone who hears these words of Mine and **acts on them** will be like a sensible man who built his house on the rock. 25 The rain fell, the rivers rose, and the winds blew and pounded that house. Yet it didn't collapse, because its foundation was on the rock.26 But everyone who hears these words of Mine and **doesn't act on them** will be like a foolish man who built his house on the sand. 27 The rain fell, the rivers rose, the winds blew and pounded that house, and it collapsed. And its collapse was great!"*

MATTHEW 7:24 -27

Jesus warns us in this parable to be wise people who build their lives on the rock, which means relying on the word of God and obeying it. Although we should always depend on Jesus, it is not a question of *if* the storm comes but *when* the storm comes. Storms can come in many forms. Storms may encompass the painful or difficult circumstances in our life. A storm can also come in the form of temptation or sin that surrounds us, including the sins we allow to invade our attention and distract us from God.

Take the prodigal son, for instance. He demanded his inheritance from his father and ran off to a far country without his father's blessing. While the son was away, one can say he was building his house on the sand, wasting his day in debauchery and wild living. As a result of his foolishness, he ran out of money and became poor. Since the son tried to build his life without God, his life fell into ruins. If circumstances couldn't get worse, a famine came.

When the son had nothing left, he decided to return to his father's house as a servant since he no longer thought of himself good enough to be his father's son. The son returned willingly, but very likely with his head low in what one would call the walk of shame. Imagine how humiliated he felt coming back to his father, starved, empty-handed and guilty of sin. However, the father did not approach his son in dread of the son's mistakes but with excited grace to forgive and restore his repentant son. While you are still alive, it is never too late to start building your house on the rock.

The Emptiness of Building a Family Without the Lord

One way to look at Psalm 127:1 is a promise with a warning. Unless the Lord is actively involved in your relationships, everything that you are aiming to accomplish in life will crumble. You can rise early, go to work, leave late, eat well, yet still be in grief, stress, and hardship. You may be working overtime, accumulating a lot of possessions, but at the end of the day, those things will fade into ruins because the Lord is not active in watching over your home as a result of your wavering faith. In a family, unless you are laboring with the Lord, all long hard days working to accumulate provisions and material possessions are spent in vain.

"Unless the Lord builds the house, its builders labor over it in vain. Unless the Lord watches over a city, the watchman stays alert in vain."

PSALM 127:1

The *Lord* in the original language (YAWH) is the eternal covenant-keeping God. The word *build* is to build up, to develop, to edify. *House* is "family dwelling." *Vain* means futile, a disastrous result. *Watching the city* means keeping it safe and secure. The watchman is the one who stays up all night in case of danger. His work would be pointless if the Lord is not in it. Parents are viewed in two ways according to verse 1, either as building contractors or as watchmen. Can I ask you, the reader, if you are a parent, grandparent, or even a great- grandparent—how is it going? Today there remains a flood of iniquity—a culture full of violence, pornography, and destructive activities that will destroy minds, rob innocent hearts, and lead our children down the wrong path. It used to be that one had to go out and buy magazines to see pornography; now nearly all of this darkness is one touch or click away. As guides and guardians of the next generation, we must be vigilant and diligent.

> *"It is in vain that you rise up early and go late to rest,*
> *eating the bread of anxious toil;*
> *for he gives to his beloved sleep."*
> PSALM 127:2

Notice in verse 2 that it is vain to rise early. It is vain to work overtime and into the night. Oftentimes we are asking the wrong questions when it comes to relationships and families. Ambition is good, but if the Lord is not in it, ambition is dead when we ask "How are we going to live?", "How are we going to have provisions?", "How are we going to educate our children?" or "Where are we going to live?", "Where are we going to attend school?", "What college am I going to attend?" Many times, we major on the minors and minor on the majors in life.

The most important question is *why*. *Why* reveals a motive. The word *why* reveals a vision for your life and your family. Asking *why* will move you forward. We are living in a mindless culture that amuses our minds away from what is important and eternal. Why is it futile to build a life without the Lord? No provision will come from your own strength and no protection is given to those who turn away from God.

There is no provision for healthy relationships without the Lord

> *"Whoever has the Son has life;*
> *whoever does not have God's Son does not have life."*
> 1 JOHN 5:12

A person without Jesus is a person without life; a person without life is a person without light; and a person without light is a person without love. We may notice the neighbors across the street and immediately think that they won't be receptive to Jesus because their life seems prosperous. They may live in more comfortable homes, drive a nice car, have nice jobs, and have children that are honor-roll athletes.

All that is visible is only the tip of the iceberg. The other 98% of the iceberg, underwater, cannot be seen. It is not a matter of *if* but *when* the work is empty. Jesus said that without him you can do nothing. Therefore, there is no sufficient provision nor sure protection without the Lord.

There is No Protection Without the Lord

Seemingly happy families are not really happy. Let's push the button and fast forward a little bit. The watchman in Psalm 127:1 describes the position of a man on top of the wall who would warn about an approaching storm, an approaching army, or an approaching pestilence that is coming against a walled city. What the Scripture is saying is that unless the Lord is watching, their enemies are far too great for them to withstand. Therefore, we *must* have the Lord's strength and His power to protect our families.

You may look at Psalm 127 and realize it describes your family as one with purpose or, in contrast, you may look at Psalm 127 and realize that your home is futile and lacks purpose. The latter is life without Jesus. Realize that the Lord desires to be intimately involved in your life. The first thought we have emerging from the text is *futility*–what it is to build a life *without* the Lord.

Think about divorce. I've heard couples say, "We just don't love one another anymore," or "The romance is not there anymore." Please do everything you can to save your marriage. Please don't give up. It's a lot better to stay together and work it out. Jesus will prepare a fresh downpour of love in your life and in your heart. Unhealthy practices in a home often include unhealthy sarcasm, bitterness, unforgiveness, malice, and anger. We are at an all-time high of mental illness and broken relationships in our society.

I was sitting with William Johnson, our pastoral leader of local mission ministries. He was telling me about his burden for fatherlessness, "Do you realize that kids who don't have a father in their life are more than likely to be incarcerated? They are more than likely to be involved in premarital sex? They are more than likely to be involved in drug and alcohol use?"

If Jesus is not in one's home, it will unravel. The message of this Psalm is to never lose sight of what is important, particularly our near ones. Keep your eyes looking upward; do not lose sight of the path you are taking as a follower of Jesus.

Fulfillment comes when you build a life, a family, a home *with* the Lord. When the Lord is building your house, you are not laboring in vain. Because the Lord is actively building your relationships, you are not laboring in vain. The Lord is desiring to protect and provide for you. Based on this promise that the Lord desires to build your home, will you join Him?

One question that may rise from a struggling believer is this: If Jesus promises abundant life, then why don't more people have more abundant marriages, families, friendships and relationships? One way to answer this question is with another question, "How did Jesus love you?"

Jesus freely gave you his love; you didn't earn it or merit it. As you have freely received, therefore you must freely give (Matthew 10:8). If you want to truly love someone, you have to first experience love. Jesus' love includes:

- Approval

- Acceptance

- Attention

What would you have to do for God to love you more? The answer is nothing! What would you have to do for God to love you less? The answer is also nothing! God loves you with an unconditional, no-strings-attached love. If you freely receive His love, you can freely give His love to others. It doesn't matter who you are, what you've done, or the brokenness in your life. God accepts you the way you are, and He loves you enough to *not* keep you the way you are.

Acceptance is not trying to change the music or the clothes people are wearing or the habits that they are doing; it is simply accepting them and not trying to change them. You would have never stopped doing what you have done if Jesus didn't accept you. If he accepted you, how much more are we to accept one another? If you have freely received acceptance, you can freely give acceptance. For example, when is the last time you looked at your son and said out loud, "I love you just the way you are"? One way you can give the love of God to your near ones is by giving your loved ones your approval. Another way is by giving them attention.

You are the apple of God's eye (Proverbs 17:8, Zechariah 2:8). As God has given you attention, give attention to those around you. Put the phone down when present with your family, look at each other in the eyes and communicate with one another. The next generation is growing up, going to college, and many of them are unable to land jobs due to poor communications skills, which is only a symptom of the problem rooted in lack of attention and care. Allow it to start with us- as we freely receive the Lord's attention, we must freely give attention to our near ones.

"Behold, children are a heritage from the Lord,
the fruit of the womb a reward.
Like arrows in the hand of a warrior are the children
of one's youth.
Blessed is the man who fills his quiver with them!
He shall not be put to shame when he speaks with his enemies
in the gate."
PSALM 127:3-5

Talk about the Lord with your children on a hike, at the grocery store line, or on the way to ball practice. Our children are special gifts from the Lord, and He has entrusted them to us; they are on loan from heaven to us. Therefore, we are to be like mighty warriors, taking them and shooting them high, enabling them to achieve great things for God and to withstand all evil.

There is a flood of wickedness coming against this nation, a growing darkness all around us. What are we to do? We are to make our homes a safe haven, allowing our children to experience the presence of the living Jesus *beyond* church, every day of the week. We are to take them and shoot them in the face of the dragon because we can cast the darkness out by the power of God.

Building one's life on the Lord ensures you will not build it alone. Jesus is holding the yoke with you. Jesus promises, "Come to Me, all of you who are weary and burdened, and I will give you rest. All of you, take up my yoke and learn from Me, because I am gentle and humble in heart, and you will find rest for yourselves. For My yoke is easy and My burden is light" (Matthew 11:28-30). Join Jesus in living and loving others well.

Upward Discipleship Challenge:

- Go to the Kennesaw Mountain Trail Guide on Page 127. Plan a visit with any family members to Nose Creek trail and experience Psalm 127 together.

- Plan a "family fun night" each week and allow a different family member to choose the game you will play. Establish a "no phone zone" for your evening.

- Discover the top relational needs of your family and yourself. Complete the "Relational Needs Assessment Tool": **http://bit.ly/2mVLMFZ**. Begin to join Jesus in meeting real needs in your family.

- Commit to memory Psalm 127:1 and begin praying this promise for your home.

- Have a family dinner at home and enjoy meaningful conversations. Begin by having everyone respond to fun questions such as, "What would you do if you won a million dollars?" or "What would be your perfect vacation?" Progress to questions like, "When do you feel most loved?"

CHAPTER 7

The Upward Journey is to Be Enjoyed with Happiness

PSALM 128

1 *How happy is everyone who fears the Lord,*
who walks in His ways!
2 *You will surely eat*
what your hands have worked for.
You will be happy,
and it will go well for you.
3 *Your wife will be like a fruitful vine*
within your house,
your sons, like young olive trees
around your table.
4 *In this very way*
the man who fears the Lord
will be blessed.
5 *May the Lord bless you from Zion,*
so that you will see the prosperity of Jerusalem
all the days of your life
6 *and will see your children's children!*
Peace be with Israel.

How Happy Are You?

On a scale of 1 to 10, rate yourself on happiness: 1 being classified as "Helpless," 5 being "Content," and 10 being "Exuberant." As you identify where you are currently, where would you like to be?

Many would argue that God's priority for His people is not happiness, but in Psalm 128, the word *happy* is stated two times. The sayings "go well for you," "be blessed," and "the Lord bless you" are also in this psalm. The journey of a disciple is often emphasized as a journey to be endured rather than enjoyed. The saying "enjoy the journey as much as the destination" also applies to the journey as disciples of Jesus.

Find joy in the journey, knowing that the hardships will stretch His redeemed people to grow in holiness. As we progress, He gradually reveals to us glimpses of His glory on both smooth and hazardous paths. Olympic athletes have to train long and hard to compete in the Olympics; lawyers and doctors have to study long and hard for their careers; parents work long and hard to provide for their children. No matter which master you serve, the journey will be long and hard as Jesus has promised in John 16:33, "You will have suffering in this world. Be courageous! I have conquered the world!"

Biblical Happiness

Happiness comes from experiencing an inward joy. This is a challenge since we live in a world of greed, where people are always longing for more possessions, entertainment, technology, and sensual pleasures. John Calvin stated that a Christian's happiness does not consist in "ease, honors, and great wealth" or in "taking from one to satisfy another ... to increase my standard of living." When Scripture speaks about happiness, it refers to being blessed. The Hebrew word *ashre* means "blessed" or "fortunate" and is used to contrast the righteous and the wicked throughout the book of Psalms. [7] "Blessed" describes a happy state of affairs and an encouragement to revel in God's goodness.

Joy is what one experiences inwardly as a follower of Jesus; it is the result of being rescued from sin by Jesus and adopted into God's family. Joy is experienced regardless of the circumstances. Jesus went to the cross not for momentary joy but for the future joy of uniting the Father's creation to Himself (Hebrews 12:1-3). Paul experienced joy in the midst of his Roman imprisonment, as he expresses in his letter to Philippians.

For the Jewish Pilgrims, happiness filled their hearts as Psalm 128 filled their mouths with singing. They were thankful to worship in Jerusalem, not work as slaves in Egypt! They were going to experience the compassion of Yahweh, not the wrath of Baal or other pagan gods. Though they were experiencing hardships along their journey through uncomfortable climates in the desert, they persevered by singing God's word in anticipation of their destination. Along our spiritual journey, we are to praise God along the way—for what He has done in the past, so that we may enjoy Him in the present, and all the while, anticipating His promises to be fulfilled in the future. Though the Israelites were traveling to an earthly destination that God promised them, God's people under the new covenant are traveling to the New Jerusalem, which is in heaven. Our time on earth is only a journey of preparation. Are you grateful and happy that you are going to the New Jerusalem for a festival and not the gates of hell for a funeral?

Put on your Happy Feet:

Be a Disciple of Jesus who Continually Experiences "Happiness" By Learning to Live with Gratitude

BE HAPPY = BE THANKFUL

How often do you show up in the Lord's presence with a grateful heart? Most often we are like Eeyore, a pessimistic, gloomy character from *Winnie the Pooh*. May I suggest God wants us to be more like Tigger, bouncing in His presence with joy? Living in gratitude is part of obeying the Great Commandment of loving the Lord with all of your heart. How can you serve and love the Lord with all of your heart? It is by *showing up before Him with a Grateful and Happy Heart*, having "happy feet." If you think you can do more if you have more, here is a perspective from Ben Stein, "I cannot tell you … how to be rich. But I can tell you how to feel rich, which is far better, let me tell you firsthand, than being rich. Be grateful… It is the only totally reliable get rich quick scheme." [8]

> *"Serve the Lord with gladness; come before Him*
> *with joyful songs…*
> *Enter His gates with thanksgiving and His courts with praise.*
> *Give thanks to Him and praise His name."*
> PSALM 100:2, 4

Check this out! A lifestyle of grateful living has been correlated in research with a person who is:

- Content—living life in the present
- Focused on the positive more than the negative
- Humble—thinks of others
- Forgiving—easily and often
- Patient—seizing life in the moment
- Remembering the goodness of the Lord
- Generous—having freely received, freely gives
- Trusting in the Father of all good gifts

The Science of Gratitude has far-reaching benefits:

- Increases well-being mentally, emotionally, and physically
- Enables one to relationally get along well with others
- Decreases depression
- Increases motivation, team-work, and improved focus
- Incentivizes giving and forgiving
- Improves resilience from setbacks, disappointments, and even trauma

One Way to Find Happiness in the Lord is to Express Gratitude

Gratitude to God leads to a life of happiness. In light of this reality, express gratitude for your relationship with the Lord. Living a life of gratitude is imperative to the Christian life. Eugene Peterson elaborates on the implications of gratitude:

"The easiest thing in the world is to be a Christian. What is hard is to be a sinner. Being a Christian is what we were created for. The life of faith has the support of an entire creation and the resources of a magnificent redemption. The structure of this world was created by God so we can live in it easily and happily as his children ... In the course of Christian discipleship we discover that without Christ we were doing it the hard way and that with Christ we are doing it the easy way. It is not Christians who have it hard, but non-Christians." 9

The Happiness of Experiencing a Loving Relationship with the Lord

"How happy is everyone who fears the Lord, who walk in His ways!"
PSALM 128:1

"Fears the Lord" may be an expression that is synonymous with feeling in awe of God, not just believing in His existence, but earnestly considering our response to Him. Let God be as He is: majestic, holy, vast and wondrous! Our view of God will be distorted if we whittle Him down to the size of our minds or comforts. No single English word conveys every aspect of the word *fear* in this phrase. The meaning of *fear* includes worshipful submission, reverential awe, and obedient respect to the covenant-keeping God of Israel. The Old Testament use of fear often indicates awe or reverence. To fear God is to express loyalty to Him and faithfulness to His covenant. Those who fear God exhibit trust in Him, obey His commandments, obtain His protection, wisdom, and blessing. 10

Fear speaks of living with God-awareness, living in the light of His Presence. The one "who walks in his ways" may be rendered also as "a person who does what He wants him to do." [11] This means we start doing the things for which He made us, taking a certain route, following certain directions, doing specific things, and having ethical standards, moral values, spiritual disciplines, social justices and personal relationships to develop.

The Happiness of Experiencing His Daily Provisions

"You will surely eat what your hands have worked for.
You will be happy, and it will go well for you."
PSALM 128:2

"The fruit of the labor of your hands" refers to the result of your work, whether in terms of wages, crops, or food. The thought of verse 2 is that the man who obeys Yahweh's laws will earn enough from his work to provide for his needs at all times. In other words, it is saying, "The work you do will give you what you need to live" or "You will enjoy the results of your work." [12]

Consider the percentages of the world in poverty. Almost half of the world, over three billion people, live on less than $2.50 a day. At least 80% of humanity lives on less than $10 a day. More than 1.3 billion people live in extreme poverty on less than $1.25 a day. Every day, 22,000 children die from poverty. According to Pew research, 88% of Americans own a car; contrast this to Bangladesh, where only 2% report having a car. [13] Fifty million primary school-aged children have no access to education, clean water, or sanitary conditions. And 780 million have no access to improved water source. Worldwide, 2.5 billion people lack access to improved sanitation (that's 35% of the world)!

From my experiences of travel to various parts of the world, the statistics resemble what I witnessed. In India, it is common to walk through open sewers. In Romania, the average household makes $2,600 a year (one of my pastor friends who is the president of a renowned university does not even own a car). In Cuba, pastors live on $11 a month.

Reflect on the following questions to cultivate gratitude in your heart:

- Do you have clean drinking water?

- Do you have access to education?

- Do you have transportation?

- Do you have a relationship with Jesus?

- Allow gratitude to arise in your heart to the Lord!

  - For He is the Father of lights

  - For He is a good, good Father

Express Gratitude for Your Family

"Your wife will be like a fruitful vine within your house,
your sons, like young olive trees around your table."
PSALM 128:3

Picture a lush garden that is well-watered and bearing lots of fruit; this is a metaphor of how God desires our relationships to flourish. God does not long for one's life to be a diseased garden, a weed-garden, or an arid desert, but He wants it to be fruitful and vibrant. In verse 3, the psalmist compares the wife of the obedient man to a fruitful vine, meaning she blessed him by bearing children. His children are compared to young olive trees. It is possible that the psalmist had in mind "sons" and not children in general. Young olive trees are from the shoots that grow around a cultivated olive tree.

If you are married, think of how you can experience a thriving marriage. One way to take special thought of your spouse is to speak words of affirmation. Let your spouse know on a consistent basis of your love. Remember that Ephesians 4:29 instructs us to speak words that edify.

Can you think of a quality you admire or appreciate in your spouse? Is there a certain way he or she has blessed you? Express gratitude often to your spouse verbally, in writing, or publicly.

THE UPWARD JOURNEY IS TO BE ENJOYED WITH HAPPINESS

"Your sons, like young olive trees around your table.
In this very way the man who fears the Lord will be blessed."
PSALM 128:3-4

Notice how children are described as being "around the table." If your family frequently eats meals together, allow meal times to be relational building times. Look for opportunities to practice Romans 12:15 by sharing "Celebrations" and "Struggles." Allow for longer times at the dinner table so you won't be rushed. Establish "no phone zones."

For many years, I've had the blessing of having my wife and daughters sit around the table for our weekly pancake breakfast, where we set time to have enriching conversations. This practice was inspired by a father who was a Navy doctor. We may say, "I'm in a Discipleship group" but are we discipling our family? If so, how do we go about discipling our families?

Let me encourage you to first abide in Christ yourself. After you have learned from God's word, transparently share how the Lord is changing you. Share what Bible verse you are experiencing and establish times of prayer and Bible reading as a family.

Are you grateful for your family? A grateful family is a happy family. Realize there are no perfect families, only messed-up ones. God desires to show us His startling mercy! Express gratitude for your family by prioritizing time together. Have a family fun night where you play games or go for a hike together. Tell your family members how grateful you are for them. Sadly, many do not realize the value of their family members until they are no longer with them.

Express Gratitude for Life-Stages

"May the Lord bless you from Zion,
so that you will see the prosperity of Jerusalem
all the days of your life."
PSALM 128:5

The Psalmist encourages others to live in hope for the future, not in regret for the past. In spite of the darkness surrounding us or in us, there is hope for future restoration. *Zion* is originally a term for the fortified section of Jerusalem, and is used by extension for the temple and the city of Jerusalem both in the present and in the future. Zion was the proper place of worship where the Lord is depicted as blessing His people, and where the Psalmist also hints that blessing can only be fully established as the entire nation worships Yahweh appropriately in His chosen place. [14] The Psalmist is living with an expectation of good for the future. This is to be the mindset for the believer, no matter what age or stage of life.

- Happy Season—Philippians 4:8

- Dry Season or Temptation—Colossians 3:1,2

- Season of Suffering—Romans 8:18

- A Season for Everything—Ecclesiastes 3:1-13

The writer is looking forward to the future blessing and restoration of Jerusalem to God's design and full population. Are you living by faith in God's prosperity all the days of your life? God desires for every life-stage to be filled with His abundant life. For He is the Lord of your youth as well as your gray hair. As a teen, live by faith and dream of great things. As a young married adult, live by faith and experience the fullness of life. As an empty-nester, live by faith, for you will see the prosperity. As a senior adult, live by faith and hope in the Lord; realize if you are not dead, you are not done. Wherever you are in the stages of life, be grateful!

Hope for the Future Legacy

"May the Lord bless you from Zion, so that you...
will see your children's children! Peace be with Israel."

PSALM 128:5-6

The blessing includes a long life and numerous progeny. Long life and many children were key tenants of Yahweh's blessings in ancient Hebraic thought. People wanted to live long enough to see their grandchildren. Long life and descendants are considered a blessing from God, as is true in many cultures today. Just think: Where do you see your family ten to twenty years from now? Live with the end in mind, live in health (take care of your physical condition), live in a close relationship with the Lord and lead your family to experience *Shalom* as it refers to the absence of war or an all-encompassing sense of well-being and wholeness. Develop a multi-generational vision for your family as well as the church. Imparting the faith to coming generations requires the older generation to pass the faith over to younger generations. Grandparents, don't underestimate your influence on your grandchildren. Share your greatest struggles and victories. Tell them about God's faithfulness!

Here is a challenge for us from the text: Increase your level of happiness by expressing gratitude to God. You are a Disciple of Jesus on an Upward Journey. Travel with happy feet! This command to give thanks is also given in 1 Thessalonians 5:18, "Give thanks in everything, for this is God's will for you in Christ Jesus."

Remember the encounter between Jesus and the ten lepers? Even if you know the story, read it again with fresh eyes by entering Jesus' perspective:

While traveling to Jerusalem, He passed between Samaria and Galilee. [12] *As He entered a village, 10 men with serious skin diseases met Him. They stood at a distance* [13] *and raised their voices, saying, "Jesus, Master, have mercy on us!"* [14] *When He saw them, He told them, "Go and show yourselves to the priests."*

And while they were going, they were healed.[15] *But one of them, seeing that he was healed, returned and, with a loud voice, gave glory to God.*[16] *He fell facedown at His feet, thanking Him. And he was a Samaritan.*[17] *Then Jesus said, "Were not ten cleansed? Where are the nine?*[18] *Didn't any return to give glory to God except this foreigner?"*[19] *And He told him, "Get up and go on your way. Your faith has made you well."*

LUKE 17:11-19

Do you sense the disappointment in Jesus' voice over the nine lepers who did not return to give Him thanks? Will you be like the one leper to return to express your thanksgiving? Will you thank Him for giving you grace, for giving you relationships, and for giving you daily provisions? Will you express your love to the Lord with a thankful heart? Gratitude will do so much more than an antidepressant can do to produce dopamine or serotonin!

Here are ways you can get started on expressing gratitude to God. Tell Him you are grateful for:

- His provision of Salvation through Jesus

- The prayers He has answered

- A person who especially shaped or guided your life

- A celebration or high point in life

- A challenge that turned into a blessing

If you have never fallen at Jesus' feet in faith, let me invite you to come to Him! Just as He touched and cleansed sinners then, He will touch you now. You need His touch, for you are separated because of your sin. Your sin leads to brokenness. The Good News is that Jesus died for your sins, was buried, and rose again. The Gospel calls you to respond by faith in Jesus with all of your heart (Romans 10:9-10).

Upward Discipleship Challenge:

- Go to the Kennesaw Mountain Trail guide on Page 130. Read and experience Psalm 128 on one of the trails this autumn.

- Happiness is developed by cultivating a heart of gratitude to God and others. Discuss with a friend or a group: Why is it important to be happy?

- Who is in your life to whom you could express a deeper level of gratitude? Say thanks, write a note, give a gift, give a testimony.

- For what blessing from God are you especially thankful? Write it down and place it in your Bible.

CHAPTER 8

The Upward Journey Requires Perseverance

PSALM 129

1 *Since my youth they have often attacked me—*
let Israel say—
2 *Since my youth they have often attacked me,*
but they have not prevailed against me.
3 *Plowmen plowed over my back;*
they made their furrows long.
4 *The Lord is righteous;*
He has cut the ropes of the wicked.
5 *Let all who hate Zion*
be driven back in disgrace.
6 *Let them be like grass on the rooftops,*
which withers before it grows up
7 *and can't even fill the hands of the reaper*
or the arms of the one who binds sheaves.
8 *Then none who pass by will say,*
"May the Lord's blessing be on you.
We bless you in the name of Yahweh."

THE UPWARD JOURNEY REQUIRES PERSERVERANCE

Can you recall being on a long journey? I can remember sitting through long road trips with my family as a child. I would constantly ask my parents, "How much longer? Are we there yet?" A long journey requires perseverance, patience, and endurance.

The pathway of a disciple of Jesus is long. It requires obedience in a long direction; it requires for us to press upward and onward. The Psalms of Ascent are songs of victory, not of defeat. Psalm 129 speaks of attackers who did not prevail against God's people, the wicked whose ropes were cut off by God and were driven back in disgrace. The people of God were confident of the overthrow of their enemies in the future because of His deliverance in the past.

Think of past victories when the Lord gave you greater confidence of His *future* victories. Can you remember a difficult time where the Lord supported you? What are the things He taught you in this time of difficulty?

As a disciple of Jesus on the upward path, you will face opposition, but don't give up! Keep pressing onward with perseverance, for the Lord will give you victory as you face adversity. Knowing that the path is long, obedience to Jesus is required and it is worth it! First, disciples of Jesus are to press upward and onward with confidence in the Lord. Second, disciples of Jesus are to respond throughout their journey with prayer.

Press Upward & Onward with Confidence in Light of Past Victories

"Since my youth they have often attacked me—let Israel say."
PSALM 129:1

Attack speaks of treatment with hostility, to press, compress, or to be in conflict. From Israel's youth, attacks have occurred. This likely refers to the Babylonian captivity or either the pain and affliction of the cruel slave masters in Egypt for 430 years. Recall Pharaoh's orders to eliminate straw for making bricks, forcing the slaves go out and find their own straw. The oppression and hard labor was inflicted on the Hebrews solely because they belonged to another people group, ethnically and culturally. The population growth was seen as a threat to Pharaoh, who had forgotten that it was from the Hebrews (descendants of Joseph and his family) by whom Egypt survived seven years of famine. In short, it was due to racism that Pharaoh attempted genocide by diminishing the Hebrews as slaves and commanding their male babies to be thrown in the Nile.

It is easy to condemn racism in history, but more difficult to face it in the present. Why? We all have "blind spots." Today, the local church in America is segregated. Local churches are ten times more segregated than the communities that surround them and twenty times more segregated than public schools. It estimated that local churches that have not embraced ethnically diversity in their community will disappear by 2040! Beware! Many people in modern American churches resemble the prejudice of the Jews in Acts 13. The Jews were envious as the Gentiles received the same privilege of hearing the Word of God and the gift of salvation (Acts 13:42-49), for they were people who did not look like them, talk like them, or practice the same customs as them. This division caused by the Jews in Antioch led the chief leaders to expel Paul and Barnabas from their region (Acts 13:50).

As the church, remember we are a missional community. Our mission is to remove people's aloneness and to share the Gospel in order to rescue people from their fallenness. The community of the church must come alongside individuals and help those who are suffering from injustice. Whether it is human trafficking, racial injustice, abuse of children or another form of injustice that creates a burning zeal within you, don't ignore it; it could be that the Lord is placing within you a righteous anger (Matthew 5:6). Eugene Peterson gives the church a wakeup call, "Do you think of Christian faith as a fragile style of life that can flourish only when weather conditions are just right, or do you see it as a tough perennial that can stick it out through storm and drought, survive the trampling of careless feet and the attacks of vandals?"[15] Standing up for justice may sound like a noble cause. However, to make a stand and take action is not easy. Jesus promised that taking a stand for Him will come at a cost. "In fact, all those who want to live a godly life in Christ Jesus will be persecuted" (2 Timothy 3:12).

"Plowmen plowed over my back; they made their furrows long"

PSALM 129:3

This speaks of the severity of the enemy's affliction and humiliation. In this text, one can hear the lashing of the whip and the thud as it hits human flesh. In this text one can hear the flowing of the blood from bodies and the groans and cries of the ones being persecuted. *"My back"* speaks of the posterior part of the body from the neck to the end of the spine. "Plowed" speaks of cutting in, just as a plow breaks and turns over the earth. The "plowmen" likely symbolize the Egyptian or Babylonian oppressors who inflicted the beatings on the Jewish people in slavery. "They made ... long" is the length or far extent of the wounds made by the enemy. "Furrows" is the action of plowing a long shallow trench on the ground

Verse 3 also parallels the physical sufferings of our Lord Jesus Christ. He endured the betrayal of His own people, the Roman flagellation and crucifixion. The horrors of the Roman lictor inflicting punishment with a flagellum exposes the suffering of the Son of God. Yet his suffering is a reminder that "by His stripes we are healed" (Isaiah 53:5 NKJV).

Whether it occurred in Egypt with the Jewish slaves, in Western Civilization with African slaves, or with segregation in 20th century America, understand that according to Scripture, there is only *one race*, which is the *human race*. Look at Acts 17:24-27:

"The God who made the world and all things in it, since He is Lord of heaven and earth, does not dwell in temples made with hands; nor is He served by human hands, as though He needed anything, since He Himself gives to all people life and breath and all things; and He made from one man every nation of mankind to live on all the face of the earth, having determined their appointed times and the boundaries of their habitation, that they would seek God, if perhaps they might grope for Him and find Him, though He is not far from each one of us."

Do you know that the pigment of one's skin is only 2% of the person's DNA? Every person is made in the image of God and is to be cherished from the womb to the grave. Therefore, every culture and ethnicity is to be cherished (Genesis 1:26; Psalm 139). Racism is not a matter of the skin. No, racism is only a symptom of a deeper problem in one's heart. Racism is a matter of *sin*.

Another form of slavery in history that is occurring today is human trafficking. What will the local church do about it? How are we to be involved? The truth is, it is no different for a follower of Christ today in our culture! We are to speak out and care for vulnerable people who come through the doors of our churches and beyond. There are also plenty of resources that can guide individuals on how to identify traffickers, victims, and the customers who cause the increasing demand of this evil trade. The least that believers in Jesus can do is to pray, but my plea is to not settle for less and sit idle.

Be Confident of Continual Triumphs

"BUT they have not PREVAILED against me."
PSALM 129:2

"But" is an important conjunction, as it leads us to how God intervened for the Psalmist regardless of the attacker. Because of God, the Psalmist's enemies didn't succeed in fulfilling their purpose against him.[16] **When the Psalmist says that God stood up for him, the emphasis is on His dependable personal relationship. The Bible says that God sticks with us, that He is always there for us.**[17] Perseverance is not the result of our determination but is the result of God's faithfulness. We survive in the way of faith, not because we have extraordinary stamina but because God is righteous. He will strengthen us to persevere until he overthrows the oppressor in His timing.

"The LORD is righteous; He has cut the ropes of the wicked."
PSALM 129:4

© William C. Ressler

This painting by William C. Ressler displays the eternal yet divided destiny between the righteous and the wicked. The wicked oppressors of God's people are lured towards the flames only to find the justice and wrath of God Himself, who will "cut the ropes" as they suffer the eternal judgment they have chosen.

On the journey upward to heaven, obstacles will fall along the path such as temptations, spiritual warfare or hard circumstances that attempt to lure us off the path. One of my favorite parts of the 2018 Winter Olympics in South Korea was to watch cross-country snow skiing, which requires great endurance for the athletes who often collapse across the finish line.

When you are reminded of the severity of the attacks of the enemy, be confident. Press upward and onward!

Our human tendency either minimizes the wound by burying it inside or maximizes the wound by seeing our damage as bigger than God. The depth of one's wound reveals the depth of God's love to deliver, heal, restore and reconcile. The path of a disciple is long and challenging, so not only do we press upward and onward with confidence, but also in prayer.

Press Upward & Onward with Prayer

The Psalmist expresses a prayerful desire that all the enemies of Zion may be consigned to utter ruin. The motto of the Psalmist could be narrowed down to the statement, "Life is fragile. Handle it with prayer." Pray with assurance that no one has defeated the Lord.

"Let all who hate Zion be driven back in disgrace"

PSALM 129:5

"Zion" is the fortified section of Jerusalem. Zion also refers to the temple and the city of Jerusalem both in the present time and in the future. Zion will be the place where Jesus will sit on the throne of David forever! The word "disgrace" means be put to shame, to be guilty or embarrassed. The enemies of God and of His people in Zion will "be driven back," meaning God will move them back.

Pray with The End in Mind

"Let them be like grass on the rooftops, which withers before it grows up and can't even fill the hands of the reaper or the arms of the one who binds sheaves. Then none who pass by will say, "May the Lord's blessing be on you."

PSALM 129:6-8

"Grass on the rooftops" will not last in the sun without shade and will die from depletion of water and care. Likewise, the state of the wicked will become less and will reap no profit in harvest time. A passerby who sees the fate of the wicked will not wish for their prosperity or life. Why? The wicked committed a "sin unto death" (1 John 5:16,17). They are beyond the point of God's blessing.

Pray Blessings on Those Around You

"We bless you in the name of Yahweh."

PSALM 129:8

Bless one another by speaking words that edify (Ephesians 4:29). Husbands and wives, practice blessing one another in the name of the Lord. Parents, practice blessing your children. The sad reality is that many children never receive the blessing of their parents. There was a son of a state congressman who spoke at his father's funeral and said, "I hope that somehow my dad was pleased with me." His words of insecurity reveal that he had never received the blessing of his father. If you are a child, young or grown, especially with aging parents, give a blessing of gratitude to your parents. Although no parent is perfect, give them words that edify. Let them know in what ways they have blessed you.

Getting Weary?

Life presses us to pray, singleness presses us to pray, marriage presses us to pray, family presses us to pray, and friends as well as enemies press us to pray. Allow the pressures of life to press you to the floor in prayer.

The words of Psalm 129 may speak to someone who has grown weary or faint-hearted. The challenge is not giving up; ask God to strengthen you. He promises from Isaiah that He will renew the strength of those who hope in Him.

Think about the weariness of Elijah the prophet (1 Kings 19). After confronting King Ahab and Queen Jezebel on their wickedness, Elijah fled Jezebel's death threat in the desert. He felt physically exhausted, hungry, and dehydrated. He felt alone, thinking he was the only living one among the prophets whom Jezebel had not massacred. In addition to those troubles, he was discouraged to the point of death, asking God to let him die in the desert. Out of weariness, Elijah lost hope. Under his ministry, very few were repenting of their idolatry nor seeking after the God of Israel.

Many times, like Elijah, we grow tired of doing the same old work for the Lord that doesn't appear to be producing any results. It makes sense why Elijah felt physically and emotionally weak as if everything he did was in vain. Nevertheless, Elijah found rest in the desert. Not only did he find shade and gain much-needed sleep, but God sent an angel of the Lord to Elijah, who provided bread and a jar of water. The Lord strengthened Elijah and he "got up, ate, and drank. Then on the strength from that food, he walked 40 days and 40 nights to Horeb, the mountain of God" (1 Kings 19:8). It was at a mountain where Elijah heard the still small voice.

God was not finished with Elijah. Before his next task, Elijah traveled through the desert and up the mountain where he was alone with God.

Just as Elijah had to experience the upward journey to be alone with God and listen to His voice, we who are on a spiritual upward journey are to listen closely to His still small voice.

Pray to the Living Jesus. Ask Him to give you resurrection in the life of your present difficulty. In addition, ask Him to give life to your family, to your marriage, to your church, and to the homes of your community.

"And if the Spirit of Him who raised Jesus from the dead lives in you, then He who raised Christ from the dead will also bring your mortal bodies to life through His Spirit who lives in you" (Romans 8:11).

Upward Discipleship Challenge:

- Reflect on recent times of difficulty. What has the Lord taught you through difficulties? Share those insights with a friend or group.

- Meditate on the Living Jesus who revives life, as you look at Romans 8:11. Memorize this verse and experience Jesus living through you.

- Prayerfully seek to share your story of the hope with someone in your daily traffic pattern (1 Peter 3:15). Invite them to join you in worship.

CHAPTER 9

When the Road Runs Out on the Journey—There is Hope

PSALM 130

1 *Out of the depths I call to You, Yahweh!*
2 *Lord, listen to my voice;*
let Your ears be attentive
to my cry for help.
3 *Yahweh, if You considered sins,*
Lord, who could stand?
4 *But with You there is forgiveness,*
so that You may be revered.
5 *I wait for Yahweh; I wait*
and put my hope in His word.
6 *I wait for the Lord*
more than watchmen for the morning—
more than watchmen for the morning.
7 *Israel, put your hope in the Lord.*
For there is faithful love with the Lord,
and with Him is redemption in abundance.
8 *And He will redeem Israel*
from all its sins.

The cry of the Psalmist begins in a state of despair. While most of the Psalms of Ascent are songs of joy, triumph and anticipation, Psalm 130 presents the reality of the pathway running out. Have you walked on a road where it ended with a cliff or the bridge was out? It is a startling feeling filled with frustration. Dead ends usually disrupt with plans or timing. Notice in this picture that the Waihee Ridge Trail has run out for Anna in the jungle among the Pacific Ocean and the Halekala Volcano. The location in Maui, Hawaii, is a beautiful place for the path to run out!

Unfortunately, not all dead ends come with a scenic view. One morning on my way to church, my normal route was blocked because of an accident. A detour by the police mapped a way back to the main path. This also occurred when hiking the Kennesaw Mountain Park trail after a storm caused some trees to fall on the path and caused a detour. Sometimes when we are walking the Upward Pathway as a Disciple, it seems that the road comes to an end, the bridge is out, or you arrive at a steep impassable area. Nevertheless, with the Lord, hope does not run out.

"OUT OF THE DEPTHS I call to you, Yahweh!
Lord, listen to my voice;
Let Your ears be attentive to my CRY FOR HELP"
PSALM 130:1-2

The "depths" speaks of the deepest and the remotest parts. No matter how low and deep you are, God's love is deeper still! When the Psalmist asks the Lord to listen, He is asking the Lord to give special revelation of His Presence in the psalmist's situation. His "cry for help" is a humble plea for someone in authority to intervene. All of us at some point will come to a deep place where the path in life arrives at a dead end with no way out. Maybe it is the depth of the wrong choices that has led you to the bottom. Maybe it is the depth of a hurtful relationship that has led you to despair. Perhaps it is the wrong use of finances that lead you to desperation. Maybe it is a job loss and you are hurting. Likewise, the path ran out for the Psalmist.

© Fundació Gala-Salvador Dalí

Here is a painting of a bridge where the path runs out. I have a daughter who loves art and museums. While on vacation, I took her to the Salvador Dalí Museum in St. Petersburg, Florida.[18] Out of all the paintings, one that remains etched in her memory is Dalí's *The Broken Bridge* and the Dream. If you look closely at the painting, you will notice a broken bridge with vanishing figures escalating to the top while the others who seemed to have fallen off the bridge resemble faded skeletons.

Is it possible that you see yourself in this painting? Have you chased something that appears important, only to find out that bridge lacked a path? One interpretation from a Christian worldview would say that

Dalí's bridge reflects the vanity of one's life without Jesus: hopelessness, confusion, despair, and lack of direction. The Psalmist, although he knew God and loved Him, was hitting rock-bottom. The broken bridge also parallels sin's empty promises to take us somewhere it will not. There are many reasons we fall into a deep place, whether circumstantial or intentional. For the Psalmist, sin grieved his spirit into the depths.

Yahweh, if You considered sins, Lord, who could stand?

PSALM 130:3

The psalmist indicates that "the depths" are caused by sin. "Sins" are thoughts, feelings, speech, or actions which ignore something required or forbidden by God's law. The term "count" (consider) means to watch, be careful and take into strict account (Job 10:14; 14:16). This word implies a confession of the existence of sin. [19] To "stand" is to be in the right condition in the Lord's presence as opposed to the guilty sinking down in fear and self-condemnation.

If God keeps a ledger of our sin, we are doomed. We cannot save or change ourselves (Romans 3:23; Isaiah 64:6). Imagine that if you wanted to reach God, you would have to jump by yourself to heaven with no help. This is impossible! But the Good News is that God has leaped down to you in your brokenness and sin! (Romans 5:8; Hebrews 7:25; Isaiah 52:2). Though the path runs out, there is hope.

When the Path runs out,
HOPE IN GOD'S WORD

Eugene H. Peterson explains, "Hope is the opposite of desperate and panicky manipulations of scurrying and worrying. And hoping is not dreaming. It is not spinning an illusion or fantasy to protect us from our boredom or our pain. It means a confident, alert expectation that God will do what He said He would do." [20]

Where can we find a confident expectation when the road runs out? When plans don't turn out the way we expect them? Let's consider sources of hope from the text. One sure source of hope we can have from God's Word is that God forgives sins.

"BUT WITH YOU there is forgiveness so that You may be revered."

PSALM 130:4

This verse is a declaration based on fact: God forgives. *Forgiveness* speaks of the gracious act of God in which an offense is no longer held against someone. Unlike people, God forgives and forgets! He is full of grace and mercy. He never gets historical with our sin! With respect and reverence, God is considered excited to bestow grace to us.

The real God promises forgiveness – removal of the guilt and payment of sin. Have you ever been forgiven of a debt? Whether it was a financial debt or debt for wrongdoing, it is an overwhelming relief to be forgiven a debt. Eugene Peterson depicts the confidence we can have from being forgiven, "Because of the forgiveness we have a place to stand. We stand in confident awe before God, not in terrorized despair." [21]

The real God provides forgiveness. In Jesus *"we have redemption through His blood, the forgiveness of our trespasses, according to the riches of His grace"* (Ephesians 1:7). Not only is the forgiveness of sins promised in God's Word, but also the promise of answered prayer.

God Hears Prayers

When life's path seems to run out, hope in God's Word, for He hears prayer! Look again at verses 1 and 2. The Psalmist is taking his cares to the Lord with anticipation that He will come through. He called out in deep distress. He cried out for God's help. What occurred? God heard and responded to His prayers. The only prayer God does not answer is one that is not prayed:

- James 4:2 – The Lord says, "You do not have, because you do not ask."
- Jeremiah 33:3 – The Lord's invitation for you to pray - "Call to Me, and I will answer you."
- Ephesians 3:20 – God's immeasurable power is promised to be released through prayer.

God is Faithful: He Always Comes Through

I wait for Yahweh; I wait and put my hope in His word.
I wait for the Lord more than watchmen for the morning—
more than watchmen for the morning.

PSALM 130:5-6

In these two verses, "wait" speaks of looking forward to the arrival of something, indicating an eager anticipation of something certain. (The Hebrew word *qwh* is used two times in these verses).

Here is an extensive insight for the person in trouble who cries out, "But surely there is something for me to do!" The answer is "Yes, there is something for you to do, or more precisely there is someone you can be. Be a watchman." [22]

A watchman functioned as a city guard standing above the walls, alert for approaching danger. The watchman didn't do very much. Nevertheless, the watchman played an imperative role since the city depended on him for security. He is simply alert to danger and gives warnings. Certainly the night sentries guarding the walls of a city (verse 6) would know that daylight will eventually come, even though the sun takes time to rise on the horizon. [23] Just as certain as the sun will come breaking through a new day, so God's word will "break through" the darkness.

Hope In God's Character

"For there is faithful love with the LORD
and with Him is redemption in abundance."

PSALM 130:7

When the path runs out, God does not! The real God is not full of religious irrelevance, nor is he distant, disappointed, or inspecting. The Lord is relational. He desires to be known by His creation and be in fellowship with them. *Faithful love* in Hebrew is *Hesed*, which speaks of a loyal love that is faithful, steadfast, unwavering, unfailing. Hesed demonstrates God's faithfulness to His covenant. He is the God of covenant relationships as detailed in the Great Commandment to love God and love others (Mark 12:28-34).

Eugene H. Peterson notes the emphasis on God's name, "Eight times the name of God is used in the psalm. We find, as we observe how God is addressed, that he is understood as One who forgives sin, who comes to those who wait and hope for him, who is characterized by steadfast love and plenteous redemption, and who will redeem Israel. God makes a difference."

One of the ways God restores His people is through redemption. The Lord is a loving God who longs to restore. Restoration happens as He *redeems* (*padah*) us from sin's imprisonment.[24] This freedom gives us direct access to God to love Him and serve Him with our hearts, not by means of earning our way to Him. God's *abundance* pours forth "complete freedom" and "great power to redeem," reflecting His attitude and His constant willingness to save people. Salvation *from all his iniquities* includes both forgiveness of sins and deliverance from their consequences.[25]

Are you hoping in the real God when the path seems to run out? It would be difficult to trust an unreal God of misunderstanding. Sometimes we can mistake God to be unkind, unforgiving and unrelatable. Maybe a hurt remains that has formed a misguided view of God from a parent, an adult, or an authority figure who has wounded or disappointed you. In spite of what it may seem, God never walks out of your life. He never stops loving you. There is never a time when He will love you less and never a time when He will love you more. He longs to restore and rescue you!

I had a conversation with my Lyft driver on my way to the airport whose name was Brenda. She was sold into sex trafficking at age 15, coming from a broken family situation. Out of desperation, she was compelled to attend a small Baptist church in inner-city Atlanta, where she experienced the love of Jesus. Now she leads a ministry to rescue those who are victims of human trafficking. Only Jesus was able to bring Brenda out of her brokenness and give her hope. Now she is a living vessel of victory who directs others to be victors. Though her victory began at a low point, so it is with us. All of us who know Christ are living vessels of victory who direct others to be victors.

PSALM 131

> ¹ Lord, my heart is not proud;
> my eyes are not haughty.
> I do not get involved with things
> too great or too difficult for me.
> ² Instead, I have calmed and quieted myself
> like a little weaned child with its mother;
> I am like a little child.
> ³ Israel, put your hope in the Lord,
> both now and forever.

When the Path runs out, Hope in God's Care for You

Brokenness has a way of humbling us and bringing us closer to God and our near ones. Many times God places us lovingly on our backs so that we can look up to Him. As Peterson observes, "Psalm 131 is a maintenance psalm. Looking up is functional to the person of faith as pruning is functional to the gardener: it gets rid of that which looks good to those who don't know any better and reduces the distance between our hearts and their roots in God."

Write this down in your Bible: God cares for you! (1 Peter 5:7). To *experience* God's care, one must receive God's care. When the path runs out, how are you to receive God's care? There are several ways from the text.

Receive God's Care Humbly

"Lord, my heart is not proud; my eyes are not haughty.
I do not get involved with things too great or too difficult for me."
PSALM 131:1

Receive God's care humbly. Humility is listening to God's calling, submitting to His will, and depending on His strength. Philippians 4:13 must be quoted correctly. Paul did not say "I can do all things," BUT "I can do all things *through Christ* who strengthens me." Pride is attempting things God never intended for you to do. The *lofty eyes* in Psalm 131:1 are a sign of pride (Psalm 18:27), with which the Psalmist does not get *involved*—he does not "walk in" or "meddle with" **pride.**

Receive God's Care Quietly

"Instead, I have calmed and quieted myself like a little weaned child with its mother; I am like a little child."
PSALM 131:2

Submission is illustrated by the figure of a weaned child. As the child is weaned from his mother, so we still have the motions of pride in us (Matthew 18:3,4; Isaiah 11:8; 28:9). Hebrew children were often not weaned until they were three years old. There is no fear in the child because of the mother's care, so it is a tender depiction of our daily abiding in Christ.

Receive God's Care Continually

"Israel, put your hope in the Lord, both now and forever."
PSALM 131:3

Now speaks of the present. Forever speaks of the future and eternity. What day or hour of this next week will you not need the Lord? Learn to pray the song, "I Need Thee Every Hour." Practice a continual abiding in Jesus! (John 15:5).

Has the pathway you are traveling been washed out or come to an end? Many struggle with guilt and past sin. Reflect on the words of Psalm 130:3 as if you are in a courtroom setting being tried. You look around the courtroom and find you are surrounded by the familiar faces of those in your life who have shamed and condemned you. They are the faces of anger, blame, and hurt. Imagine yourself saying these words, *"Lord, if you should count sins, who can stand?"* Suddenly The Judge walks into the courtroom. Instead of being intimidated by his entrance, you notice something different. He is gracious and kind. He looks at you with care and compassion. Reflect on the words of Psalm 130:4, *"But with you there is forgiveness so that You may be revered."*

This Judge takes off his robe, pays for your penalty and then assumes his robed position on the bench. He declares you not guilty. Reflect now on the words of Romans 8:33,34 with a courtroom faded in the background of the judge's bench:

"Who can bring an accusation against God's elect?
God is the One who justifies.
Who is the one who condemns?
Christ Jesus is the One who died,
but even more, has been raised;
He also is at the right hand of God
and intercedes for us."

Do you sense God's loving embrace of you? Express your heart in prayer to Him now.

Upward Discipleship Challenge:

- Go to the Kennesaw Mountain Trail Guide on Page 132. Take a visit to the Hardage Mill Loop and experience Psalm 131.
- Prayerfully read Psalm 130. How might this text lead you to encounter and love the Real God? Express your love to God by writing out a prayer.
- Prayerfully read Psalm 131. How might this text affirm your identity as His Beloved? Discuss with someone.
- Who could benefit from hearing your life story of encountering hope in Jesus? Be ready to give an answer for the reason of hope within you (1 Peter 3:15).

AN UPWARD PATH
OF A DISCIPLE

CHAPTER 10

The Upward Journey Requires a Long Obedience in the Same Direction

PSALM 132

¹ *Lord, remember David*
and all the hardships he endured,
² *and how he swore an oath to the Lord,*
making a vow to the Mighty One of Jacob:
³ *"I will not enter my house*
or get into my bed,
⁴ *I will not allow my eyes to sleep*
or my eyelids to slumber
⁵ *until I find a place for the Lord,*
a dwelling for the Mighty One of Jacob."
⁶ *We heard of the ark in Ephrathah;*
we found it in the fields of Jaar.
⁷ *Let us go to His dwelling place;*
let us worship at His footstool.
⁸ *Rise up, Lord, come to Your resting place,*
You and Your powerful ark.
⁹ *May Your priests be clothed with righteousness,*
and may Your godly people shout for joy.

¹⁰ *Because of Your servant David,*
do not reject Your anointed one.
¹¹ *The Lord swore an oath to David,*
a promise He will not abandon:
"I will set one of your descendants on your throne.
¹² *If your sons keep My covenant*
and My decrees that I will teach them,
their sons will also sit on your throne forever."
¹³ *For the Lord has chosen Zion;*
He has desired it for His home:
¹⁴ *"This is My resting place forever;*
I will make My home here
because I have desired it.
¹⁵ *I will abundantly bless its food;*
I will satisfy its needy with bread.
¹⁶ *I will clothe its priests with salvation,*
and its godly people will shout for joy.
¹⁷ *There I will make a horn grow for David;*
I have prepared a lamp for My anointed one.
¹⁸ *I will clothe his enemies with shame,*
but the crown he wears will be glorious."

This is a Prayer for the Ark of the Covenant to find a resting place. In the Old Testament, the ark represented God's power, presence and provision for His obedient redeemed people. It was a visible sign of the invisible God who dwelled in Israel's midst. 26 Another title of the ark is known as the "Ark of Testimony." The Ark of the Covenant first dwelt in the Tabernacle as a portable earthly dwelling of God among the children of Israel from the time of the Exodus to the conquest of Canaan.

This Psalm of Ascent would be sung by the Jewish pilgrims going up to the Temple, to a feast of gratitude. Looking ahead, the Temple was built and completed in the time of Solomon, destroyed in the Babylonian exile (586 B.C.), rebuilt after the return of the exiles (500 BC), then redesigned during the Herodian rule under Rome in time for the Messiah's coming. Further, this Psalm of Ascent would be sung by Jesus and His disciples as they would travel to the Jewish feast in His earthly ministry (see John 2:13, 5:1)

Verses 1-6: Background of the Ark & Israel's Kings

Psalm 132 is likely written from the perspective of Solomon or an unknown writer from the era of Solomon. Solomon would have prayed the prayer of Psalm 132 in anticipation of building the first Temple in Jerusalem.

Before Solomon would become the third king of Israel, recall how Saul, the first king of Israel, lost his kingdom out of failure to obey the Lord's commands. David, the second king of Israel, received success and blessings as a man after God's own heart. His dream was to build a Temple for the Ark of God to dwell instead of a large tent. The Ark had been in Ephrathah, a location containing several villages, including Bethlehem and Kiriath-jearim ("City of woods") [27] where the ark of the covenant was housed for a time before it was brought to Zion [28] (1 Samuel 7:1; 2 Samuel 6:3,4). In his sleeplessness, David was eager to fulfill this dream and prayed.

When the king had settled into his palace and the Lord had given him rest on every side from all his enemies, the king said to Nathan the prophet,
"Look, I am living in a cedar house while the ark of God sits inside tent curtains."
So Nathan told the king, "Go and do all that is on your heart, for the Lord is with you."
2 SAMUEL 7:1-3

Verses 7-16: Solomon Continued the Prayer for the Permanent Placement of the Ark

The Lord responds by giving a promise to David in 2 Samuel 7:11-16, allowing David's descendant (Jesus) to sit on His throne over an eternal kingdom! Yet it would be David's son who would build the Temple and not David himself. As King Solomon sat on the throne, he remembered the prayer of his father's heart to build the Temple as a physical dwelling place for the ark. Solomon came to the throne after David, filled with the wisdom of God and blessed by God with abundant riches. This Psalm is Solomon's prayer for God's promise to David to be fulfilled.

This Psalm has terrific prophetic implications for the present and for the future time when the City of Jerusalem will be new. In addition, there is the promise that a descendant of King David will reign on His eternal throne (Revelation 19-21). One insightful commentary on Psalm 132 covers the text's meaning in the context of a temporary ancient kingdom and the eternal kingdom:

"The writer, perhaps Solomon (compare Ps. 132:8,9), after relating David's pious zeal for God's service, pleads for the fulfilment of the promise (2 Sa. 7:16), which, providing for a perpetuation of David's kingdom, involved that of God's right worship and the establishment of the greater and spiritual kingdom of David's greater Son. Of Him and His kingdom both the temple and its worship, and the kings and kingdom of Judah, were types. The congruity of such a topic with the tenor of this series of Psalms is obvious." [29]

This Psalm aims to fill our hearts before the Lord with gratitude that He fulfilled His promise to David and to fill our hearts with anticipation that His future promise will be fulfilled (2 Timothy 3:16; Matthew 22:39,40). This prayer is for Jerusalem, a city with historical significance.

The future promises are in Psalm 132:13-14, where God's desired home for the new Jerusalem is where He has destined our King Jesus Christ to reign for eternity. One may wonder how long it will take for the future throne (New Jerusalem) to come to fulfillment. We are living in the last days before the rapture of the church, the Great Tribulation, the Second Coming of Jesus, the Millennial Reign, the Great White Throne and the Eternal State. No one knows the day or the hour in which Jesus will return, but we wait in faith, knowing God fulfills his promises like he did to David (Matthew 24:36).

Note that the timeline below represents one out of a few eschatological interpretations from the book of Revelation. Some Christians believe the rapture will happen before the tribulation while others believe it will happen during or after the tribulation. No matter which view of the end times a person holds in the placement of the rapture's timing, what matters is that everyone should live in light of the end times, believing that the Lord will fulfill what He says will come to pass.

Timeline of the End Times

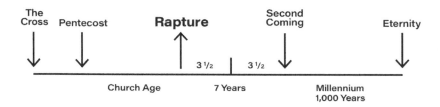

The Present & The End Times

What does this mean for disciples of Jesus today? While the Church waits for the second coming of Jesus, let me remind you that there is nothing instantaneous about being a disciple of Jesus. Disciples are constantly stepping upward with progress, weariness, perseverance, and

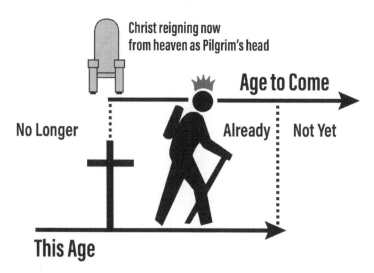

focus (Colossians 3:1-2). Psalm 132 aims to raise anticipation among God's people while maintaining their long obedience in the same direction. All who follow Jesus as Lord will enter heaven, then we will one eternal day reign with the Lord.

Be Long In Obedience, for God Fulfills His Promises

Without God's promises to David, there is no eternal Savior on the throne. This has everything to do with the present. The church would cease to exist without God's promises throughout history.

Image: Model of Solomon's temple. The Ark rested in the Temple for over 436 years, from Solomon's reign until 586 B.C.— the Babylonian Captivity.

What can we experience from this text? God is faithful to His promises. "Faithful is He who calls you, who also will do it" (1 Thessalonians 5:24). From His faithfulness we can have assurance if we depend on Him. Here are a few passages that describe God's faithfulness:

- Philippians 1:6 — *"I am sure of this, that He who started a good work in you will carry it on to completion until the day of Jesus Christ."*
- Joshua 23:14 — *"I am now going the way of all the earth, and you know with all your heart and all your soul that none of the good promises the Lord your God made to you has failed. Everything was fulfilled for you; not one promise has failed."*

- Philippians 4:19 — *"And my God will supply all your needs according to His riches in glory in Christ Jesus."*
- Hebrews 13:5 — *"Your life should be free from love of money. Be satisfied with what you have, for Himself He has said, "I will never leave you or forsake you.""*

Verses 17-18: Anticipate Prayers to be Answered Based on the Promises of God's Word

Over numerous years and many prayers, God blessed Solomon with abundant riches to construct the temple, a beautiful sacred sanctuary for the Ark of God to rest on Mount Zion! Though the temple was not constructed during David's lifetime, he tenaciously devoted himself in prayer for its completion. What can be applied from David and Solomon's life of prayer is that our repeated prayers, long days and long years of praying, waiting, surrendering our wants in obedience will bring about long-term blessings. In spite of how vacant our prayers feel on our lips and spirit, persist in them with perseverance.

Consider the prophet who anointed David as King. Samuel's ministry and existence began as an answer to his mother's prayer:

Oh, GOD-of-the-Angel-Armies,
If you'll take a good, hard look at my pain,
If you'll quit neglecting me and go into action for me
By giving me a son,
I'll give him completely, unreservedly to you.
I'll set him apart for a life of holy discipline.[30]

A woman named Hannah was barren and prayed for a child. In pain and in desperation, she promised the Lord she would dedicate her child's life to His service. One year later, God blessed Hannah with her firstborn, Samuel, who would become the last judge of Israel and one of Israel's most faithful prophets.

When Hannah carried Samuel to the sanctuary of Shiloh to fulfill her vow, she approached Eli the priest with joy, "Excuse me, sir. Would you believe that I'm the very woman who was standing before you at this very spot, praying to GOD? I prayed for this child, and God gave me what I asked for" (1 Samuel 1:25-26, The Message). Whether God would have us wait a day, a year, or beyond our lifetime, He delights in answering our prayers. In praying and waiting for an answer, God's timing is perfect.

Take your Bible in your hand and express your faith to God and His Word, "Lord, I believe all of your Promises are true, and I trust in Your Word." Remembering the practical encouragements of the Psalms causes anticipation to rise in our hearts, so that we can maintain a long obedience in the same direction.

The Bible is a Book of Prophecy. There is no other holy book like the Bible that is full of foretelling the future and fulfilling the promises. The past faithfulness of God to fulfill His promises and the many prophecies fulfilled in the first coming of Jesus (see the book of Matthew) gives us confidence that the Lord will keep His Word. Look at the prophecies and promises that came to pass from Psalm 132:13-18:

Verses 13-18: This came to fulfillment in Solomon's day and it will also come to pass in the Eternal Day.

Verses 13-14: The Lord did choose Jerusalem as His worship site and He will bless the city and keep His promise to David.

Verse 15: The Lord feeds the impoverished through the bread given from Zion.

Verse 16: The joy of salvation was experienced from Zion.

Verse 17: *"I will make a HORN grow for David. I have prepared a lamp for My anointed one."* The horn is a symbol of strength and help, which would occur from God to David's descendants. The lamp is a figure of prosperity and the unceasing splendor of the Crown from David's Line.

When Jesus was born, he was born as the legitimate descendant of David. See the genealogies of Matthew 1 as well as the angel's announcement to Mary that her Son would sit on throne of David forever in Luke 2. When Jesus was on earth, he would have visited the Temple numerous times with his family or his disciples while singing the Psalms of Ascent as they were traveling (as was the custom of Jews in that century). Jesus claimed to be the Temple (John 2:18–22), to be the Light of the world (John 8:12), to be the Source of Living Water and to be our Salvation (John 7:37–39). Jesus also foretold the coming destruction of Jerusalem that would take place in A.D. 70:

As He approached and saw the city, He wept over it, [42] *saying, "If you knew this day what would bring peace—but now it is hidden from your eyes.* [43] *For the days will come on you when your enemies will build an embankment against you, surround you, and hem you in on every side.* [44] *They will crush you and your children within you to the ground, and they will not leave one stone on another in you, because you did not recognize the time of your visitation."*

LUKE 19:41-44

Jesus died and rose again, fulfilling the promise that salvation would come from Zion! Yet presently, the Temple Mount is desolate. Though the Dome of the Rock rests there now, that is not where the story ends. When Jesus returns the second time, He will be wearing a crown and *"will clothe His enemies with shame but the crown He wears will be glorious"* (Psalm 132:18, Revelation 19). He will reign from Zion for 1,000 years, leading to the Great White Throne Judgment and the Eternal State (Revelation 20). He will be the Alpha and the Omega. This chapter in Revelation foretells the total fulfillment of prophecy,

Then I saw a new heaven and a new earth, for the first heaven and the first earth had passed away, and the sea no longer existed. I also saw the Holy City, new Jerusalem, coming down out of heaven from God, prepared like a bride adorned for her husband. Then I heard a loud voice from the throne: Look! God's dwelling is with humanity, and He will live with them. They will be His people, and God Himself will be with them and be their God.

He will wipe away every tear from their eyes. Death will no longer exist; grief, crying, and pain will exist no longer, because the previous things have passed away.

REVELATION 21:1-4

Our Lord Jesus taught us to pray, "Your kingdom come ... on earth as it is in heaven." On that day, the Lord's prayer will be answered. Jesus will come again with great power and glory, where we will forever be with the Lord in a New Heaven, a New Earth, and a New Jerusalem. The Lord will be our Temple!

How Should We Live Today?

The challenge is to live in obedience and keep praying, for if God answered prayers in the past, He is trustworthy to answer prayers in the future! There is nothing short or easy about the journey as a disciple of Jesus. Take for instance, the first disciples of Jesus. They followed Him on earth for three years, experiencing the challenges of his ministry, going through the uncertainty of His death, and witnessing the supernatural appearance of His resurrection and His ascension. Following Christ's ascension, they preached the Gospel in the 1st century. Nearly all of them were martyred. Approximately 2,000 years has passed since Jesus ascended into heaven, yet He will come again (John 14:4; 2 Peter 3:9-11; Revelation 1:11; Acts 1:9-11)! We are living in the last days, so don't give up or grow weary in well-doing (Galatians 6: 9)! Posture yourself with prayer, obedience, and anticipation. Be faithful and content while waiting.

In light of God's promise to David, in light of Jesus who died on the cross, and in light of Him who rose from the dead and will come again, live confidently. Live humbly, live prayerfully, live alert. The harvest will cease to grow if people merely acknowledge the word of God but fail to obey it. Here are two primary teachings of Jesus we are to obey as it aligns with the rest of Scripture: The Great Commission (Matthew 28:18–20) and the Great Commandment (Matthew 22:35–40). In a nutshell, these two commandments are love the Lord and love your near ones.

The mission statement of the church is "To make disciples of Jesus who love God, love people and lead others to do the same." What does this look like? Be clear and intentional in following Jesus while inviting others to follow Him.

Upward Discipleship Challenge:

- Discuss with a friend or group: Why does being a disciple of Jesus require obedience?
- Read Psalm 132:7-8 and make this your prayer. Express your worship to the Lord by showing up in His presence with a joyful and humble heart.
- Pray for individuals along your path and invite them on the upward journey as a disciple. Look for opportunities to "give first" and share your hope in Jesus.
- Encourage a friend or family member with the words of Hebrews 12:1, "Let us run with endurance the race." Invite them to join you for worship.

HE UPWARD JOURNEY REQUIRES A LONG OBEDIENCE IN THE SAME DIRECTION

CHAPTER 11

The Upward Journey is Never to be Traveled Alone—Always Together!

PSALM 133

1 *"How good and pleasant it is*

when brothers live together in harmony!

2 *It is like fine oil on the head,*

running down on the beard,

running down Aaron's beard

onto his robes.

3 *It is like the dew of Hermon*

falling on the mountains of Zion.

For there the Lord has appointed the blessing—

life forevermore."

Upward Together: Expressing the Beauty of Unity

"How good and pleasant it is
when brothers live together in harmony!"

PSALM 133:1

The spiritual journey in Christ is not intended to be made alone. The verb in Hebrew translated *"to live"* means "to sit" or "to live together." "Living together in harmony" usually implies a communal meal as part of the festival and worship gathering. [31] This thought was appropriate for the religious festivals when Israelite families would come together and worship their Lord.[32]

Psalm 133 puts into a song what is said and demonstrated throughout Scripture in the church; community is essential. Scripture knows nothing of the solitary Christian. People of faith are always members of a community. [33] Jesus worked with His disciples and lived with them in community. The church was formed when 120 people were "all together" in one place (Acts 2:1; 5:12). When some of the early Christians were dropping out of the community and pursuing private interests, a pastoral leader wrote to them, urging them to nurture their precious gift of community, "not avoiding worshiping together as some do but spurring each other on, especially as we see the big day approaching" (Hebrews 10:25, The Message). Not only do the people of God *worship* together, but they also *serve* one another. Nehemiah didn't rebuild the walls and gates around Jerusalem as one man. He was surrounded with a community who rolled up their sleeves and began the work with him, contributing towards the restoration of their community.

Does harmonious living mean that we have no differences? Of course not. In families, communities, cultures, and the church, differences are inevitable. Unity means we set aside differences and preferences that are not edifying in order to love one another and worship together! Unity is like a rug which from the bottom has a bunch of knots and strings, but on the top, it is a beautiful mosaic tapestry! The exhortation of this text is about traveling upward together.

Experiencing the Benefits of Unity

"It is like fine oil on the head, running down on the beard,
running down Aaron's beard onto his robes.
3 It is like the dew of Hermon falling on the mountains of Zion."
PSALM 133:2-3

The anointing oil for the high priest was made from olive oil mixed with four of the best spices (Exodus 30:22,25,30). Its rich profusion typified the abundance of the Spirit's graces. One commentator suggests that the oil gave off "the pervasive influence of good will." [34] The Psalmist speaks of an oil that is designated to anoint a person as a priest. To "live together in harmony" is compared to fine oil flowing over the head, down the face, through the beard, and onto the shoulders of each other. To know that you are among God's anointed is to become refreshed and renewed. When we see one another as God's anointed, our relationships are profoundly affected. [35]

"The dew of Hermon" symbolizes Yahweh's provision for the land of Israel. Dew was often a crucial source of water. [36] The alpine dew communicates a sense of morning freshness, a feeling of fertility and a clean anticipation of growth. Important in any community of faith is an ever-renewed expectation in what God is doing with our brothers and sisters in the faith. [37] The dew of vegetation was a fitting symbol of the Lord's blessing on His people. [38] As the abundant dew falls from the mountains of Zion, so is unity fruitful in good works.

Expecting Heaven's Blessing upon Unity

"For there the Lord has appointed the blessing– life forevermore."
PSALM 133:3

The blessing of Zion may also suggest the source of the influence enjoyed by the spiritual Zion, which is the church. [39] Psalm 133 instills just a hint of heaven since the rousing good fellowship will be in heaven forever. Where relationships are warm and expectancies fresh, we are already beginning to enjoy the life together that will be completed in our lives for eternity.

"The blessing" is talking about heaven, with a unified Church. The blessing is withheld from a divided local church, however. A divided Church will fall and fail for the testimony of the Gospel in its own community. Only Jesus is the Source of our unity. When the church places Jesus as the focus of worship and fellowship, a church can stand united for the testimony of the Gospel within its own city. A unified church of differing generations and cultures testfies that Jesus is the Savior of both Jews and Gentiles; He is the God of all nations and the Savior of the World!

Jesus is pleased with unity in the midst of diverse generations, cultures, ethnicities, and economic conditions. Do you know that Jesus intercedes on our behalf for the unity of believers? The night before he was crucified, He prayed, "May they be made completely one, so the world may know You have sent Me and have loved them as You have loved Me" (John 17: 23). Through this prayer, Jesus is leading His Church in unity before it was ever formed.

As the church follows Jesus in unity, beware of a gathering that calls itself the church while confusing unity for uniformity. Perils plague a church that maintain uniformity, where everyone must dress the same way, talk the same way, vote the same way, read the same version of the Bible, or have the same economic, educational, and cultural background.

The pressure of uniformity comes in many forms. It can come in the form of showing partiality to a circle of good friends and influential people while ignoring the lonely. It may look like tolerating and embracing those with unrepentant sin while condemning others on a path to repentance because their sins are somehow considered less tolerable. The route of defining others as problems to be solved is the way one might repair an automobile. However, this is not the way the body of Christ is to build one another up. People who make up the church body gather in the name of Jesus through whom all things hold together (Colossians 1:17).

Unity must be pursued and Spirit-prompted since it does not come naturally. Imagine a multigenerational family having a meal together (grandmother, parents, teen, child). There's a teen in the room who is busy playing video games, but he doesn't want to come because he dislikes meatloaf. Regardless of the teen's resistance, his parents instruct him to come because he is part of the family. Early on, the parents want their teen and small child to know there is more to mealtime than eating. Family dinner is not about the food; it's about the family. Let's mix this scenario up: for the next dinner, pizza is served. Grandmother does not prefer pizza for digestive reasons, but she comes to the table. She treasures the time she has to be in the presence of her family and impart wisdom to them. Of course, she may prepare herself another meal and sit down with them, yet at the end of the day, Grandmother is not there for the food but for the family.

In the family of faith, there are things you will not like, yet thank God you have a seat at the table! As it is wrong for a family member to reject the table due to food preferences, so it is wrong for a member of Christ's church to reject the table because preferences or demands are not being met, resembling the attitude of an immature adolescent who likes to play video games instead of being together as a family.

Community and unity are essential to the upward journey of a disciple. Although Jesus is the son of God, He did not live His earthly life in solitude. He did take time to be alone in prayer, yet he had a community of twelve disciples and other followers with whom to grow. Darkness will overtake disciples of Jesus when they are alone. Jesus invites us to his table – come and eat of His bread and drink from His cup! We have a seat in the family of God, but imagine what it will be like when we sit at the marriage supper of the Lamb! Picture the faces of the saints throughout history and around the world all at one table, sitting before the face of Jesus.

"Our community with one another consists solely
in what Christ has done to both of us."
DIETRICH BONHOEFFER

Upward Discipleship Challenge:

- Read the Kennesaw Mountain Trail on page 135. Take a hike up Little Kennesaw with a friend or a small group and experience Psalm 133.
- Pray Psalm 133 for the relationships closest to you. Commit these verses to memory.
- Look for the opportunities to enjoy fellowship outside of the usual Sunday morning experience. Invite someone to coffee or a meal.
- Look for opportunities to invite someone who is alone to join you on the Upward Journey in worship and life group.

CHAPTER 12

The Upward Steps in a Long Journey Culminates in BLESSING

PSALM 134

1 *"Now praise the Lord,*
all you servants of the Lord
who stand in the Lord's house at night!
2 *Lift up your hands in the holy place*
and praise the Lord!
3 *May the Lord,*
Maker of heaven and earth,
bless you from Zion."

This final Psalm of Ascent comes to an end with a blessing. Verses 1 and 2 encourage us, the worshipers, to bless the Lord by expressing our love to Him. Verse 3 is an exhortation to bless others and express love to those near us. We know that the demonstration of love and care towards God and other people does not come naturally for us, but we are empowered by the Holy Spirit. A good definition of a disciple of Jesus is simply "one who serves." Disciples of Jesus are ones who serve the Lord (Acts 13:1), serve His Word (Acts 6: 4), serve one another (Galatians 5:13) and serve His Mission (2 Corinthians 5:18-19).

Let's observe how to be a disciple who serves. The basic teaching from our Lord about our relationship with Him and one another is found in His Great Commandment, *"Love the Lord your God with all your heart, with all your soul, and with all your mind. This is the greatest and most important command. The second is like it: Love your neighbor as yourself. All the Law and the Prophets depend on these two commands."* (Matthew 22:35–40).

Minister to the Lord with Blessing
Psalm 134:1-2

As His disciples, loving the Lord is the *first priority*. In order to Love the Lord with all your heart, mind, soul, and strength, it is important to have an accurate view of God. Grievously, there are major misunderstandings of God. Perhaps it is from a painful past or from people who promote irrelevant religion.

For instance, when you read these words of Jesus, *"If you love Me, you will keep My commands,"* how do you view His face? How do you hear His tone of voice? How do you see His posture? I'm pained to think of the people I know and love dearly who have been misled to see a *finger-pointing, inspecting Jesus*. Some may see a disappointed Jesus with a solemn face. Some may see a *distant Jesus* who says these words with His back to them, walking out the door. Some may see an *inspecting Jesus*, who is looking for any opportunity to confront their sins. But the Biblical context of Jesus' words are a promise, *"Because you love Me (as an outcome of our deep friendship), you will keep My commands."*

The real God is the One found in the pages of the Bible. He is the One who pursues a relationship with His created ones in His image by the work of Jesus' reconciliation on the cross (2 Corinthians 5:17-18). He is the One who provides second chances and is patient with us (2 Peter 3:9). He is the One who provides redemption through the promised Messiah. He is the One who is excited to show us grace (Isaiah 30:18). He is the One who sings over us with shouts of joy (Zephaniah 3:17). He is the One who has opened arms to receive us (Luke 19:1-11). He is the One who weeps with us in our pain (John 11:35). He is the One who prays for us (John 17). He is the One who meets our needs (Philippians 4:19). He is the One who reveals Himself to relate with us – YAHWEH.

This real God who is revealed in the pages of the Word is the One whom you can love as the first priority. Let's see how the Psalmist blesses the Lord by ministering to Him.

Songs & Spoken Words

"Now praise the Lord, all you servants of the LORD."

PSALM 134:1

"Praise the Lord" or "Bless the Lord" means to speak words of excellence about Him in the form of kneeling and praising Him in His presence. *LORD* in Hebrew is Yahweh (YHWH). What words of praise can you give to the Lord? Here are some attributes to start you off:

- His Love

- His Sovereignty

- His Providence

- His Justice

- His Majesty

Reflect back on the songs, hymns, and spiritual songs that you may have sung with your church family. What words of praise did we sing to God? Another way to minister to the Lord is to speak with Him, whether it is in prayer or in song. Praise God for the things you appreciate about Him and tell Him the matters of your mind while yielding to His Word. In other words, pray with a willingness to obey where He leads you with your prayers. Notice how the Psalmist refers to the people of God as *servants of the LORD*, which speaks of someone's humility and respect under the authority of God.

With Anticipation & Steadfastness

"Who stand in the LORD'S house at night!"

PSALM 134:1

Stand means to go up before the Lord. The *LORD'S House* was the Temple or local residence of God among the people. Look at the time at which the servants of God would go to the Lord's house. They would stand at night!

When I had the opportunity to open the US Congress in prayer, I recall standing on the speaker's podium where so many presidents and leaders have stood. Though there was an overwhelming sense of honor and respect in that place, none of it compares to entering the presence of God. There is no place more important than to stand before the Lord's presence in worship!

During the rest of our time in Washington DC, my wife and I went to the Arlington National Cemetery, where we watched the changing of the guard at the Tomb of the Unknown Soldier. The tomb is guarded 24 hours a day, 365 days a year in all kinds of weather conditions. If that is true of our military giving honor to the dead, how much more should we be steadfast in the worship of our living Lord? I urge you not to miss out on being still before the Lord.

With Outward Expression

"Lift up your hands in the holy place and praise the Lord!"

PSALM 134:2

Lift up your Hands – speaks of raising, to raise from lower to higher the extremity of the arm from the wrist to the fingers. The *holy place* is a place consecrated for God to dwell and to be worshipped. To praise is to bless, bow, or speak words of excellence about someone. Whether you are an expressive worshipper or a contemplative worshipper, the Lord is pleased to receive praise from His creation; He delights in it! Worship sets our minds and hearts above. It is a part of leading your heart to love the

Lord rather than following your heart.

One of the greatest battlefields is fighting for your heart. Not only is the heart easily deceived but it is desperately wicked (Proverbs 4:25, Jeremiah 17:9, John 4:24,25). Unless a person submits his/her heart to Jesus, it will remain evil, deceived, restless, and in despair. The mind and the heart are shaped by one's habits– to whom or what you give of your time, efforts, and allegiance. James K. A. Smith points to the heart imperative as he emphasizes, "Our habits thus constitute the fulcrum of our desire: they are the hinge that 'turns' our heart, our love, such that it is predisposed to be aimed in certain directions." [40]

A habit is a statement without words. Imagine if all believers fostered a habit of worship, how different would our lives be? It is alone compelling that a body of believers worship together once or twice a week, but how about in your daily life only between you and God? Expressive worship may look like bowing your knees in prayer or writing your praises in a journal. I also put on worship music in my car or while I am getting ready for work in the mornings. Once or twice a week, I like to go on prayer walks down the Cheatham Hill trail behind my neighborhood and pour out my praises and petitions to God– sometimes I do this with my family. There are a variety of ways to worship. If you are extremely expressive, maybe you want to dance in your living room!

Worship the Lord even when you don't feel like it. Worship is not only good medicine for the soul, but it is a necessary discipline. One reason the pilgrims would have harmonized this Psalm on their ascent to Jerusalem is to remind themselves that in spite of the challenges, there is One who is worthy. Praising the Lord is not pretending that problems are non-existent. In prosperity and in tribulation, praising God redirects one's focus on the big picture. Without a habit of worship, forgetfulness and busyness blind us from experiencing a thriving relationship with God and our effectiveness for the kingdom of heaven is minimized.

You must lead your heart because our hearts are easily distracted by busyness. Remember the story of Mary and Martha? Recall Jesus' words of affirmation for His friend, Mary, as she was seated at His feet, listening to His words: *"Mary has chosen that good part, which will not be taken away from her"* (Luke 10:42). [41] Mary, much like the Samaritan leper of Luke 17, humbly longed to relate to Jesus.

Faithful, maturing followers of Jesus sit humbly at His feet, giving careful deep consideration to Him. This lifestyle, though empowered by His Spirit, must be chosen. Disciples never "stumble into" maturity. The transforming process of encountering Jesus must be chosen, sought after, and pursued. The Psalmist expressed this chosen pursuit: "As a deer longs for streams of water, so I long for You, God. I thirst for God, the living God. When can I come and appear before God?" (Psalm 42:1-2).

As this thirst develops in us as followers of Jesus, we come to view times of prayer, worship, meditation, fellowship, and study of the Word as privileged opportunities to pursue and encounter Jesus at the point of His Word. Through these times, our relationship with Him deepens as the past and present connections are etched on our hearts, always ready to be recalled and embraced.

Consider for a moment some special memories that you have of encountering Jesus:

I recall the time when _____ . Pause to give thanks.

Consider also significant images of Jesus you have encountered in Scripture as He prays for you (Hebrews 7:25) and as He expresses compassion for your hurts and griefs (John 11:35).

A significant encounter Jesus I have experienced is when _____ .

We are observing how to be a disciple who serves both vertically to the Lord and horizontally to one another. We minister to the Lord and to one another with a blessing. As you experience the startling love of the Lord in "loving you first," you can express the startling love of the Lord in "giving first to others."

Minister to the Near Ones by Blessing
Psalm 134:3

"May the LORD, Maker of heaven and earth,
BLESS YOU FROM ZION."

PSALM 134:3

Bless you invokes a divine favor, implying a positive disposition or kind actions towards the recipient. The Authority from which this blessing is invoked is from the Creator of the heavens and the earth. The intent of God's blessing is to show kindness towards us. As God has ministered to us, so we are to minister to those around us.

When is the last time you ministered to the ones closest to you with a blessing? If you are married, bless your spouse. Bless your children, your parents, your friends, your church, your co-workers, your boss, your teacher, your fellow classmates. As a father, this is a game-changer in your children's life. Blessing one another is a powerful and transformational practice. How can you minister to your near ones? Love one another as Jesus has loved you. One way to love people is by meeting their relational needs.

Here is a list of ten relational needs you can meet in the lives of your near ones:

Ten Relational Needs

Acceptance	Comfort
Affection	Encouragement
Appreciation	Respect
Approval	Security
Attention	Support

Acceptance

The need for acceptance is met when someone likes you even though you're different. Acceptance isn't trying to change or fix someone. When someone accepts you, that person loves you even when you mess up; he or she gives you a second chance. It sounds like this: *"I love you just the way you are!"* or *"I'm glad I'm your husband/wife even when you mess up."*

Affection

The need for affection is met by *giving hugs, kisses, pats on the back, putting an arm around someone or sitting close to someone.* It sounds like this: *"You're really special! I love you."*

Appreciation

The need for appreciation is met when *someone recognizes your accomplishment or effort*—especially noticing the things you have done and shares their thanks. Appreciation is often given through certificates, medals, or trophies. It sounds like: *"You did a terrific job on the yard!"* *"Thank you for working hard and pitching in with the project," "You played a great game last night!"*

Approval

The need for approval is met when you are bragged on through word of mouth—especially for the kind of person you are, not just the things you do. Approval is given when someone *affirms your character* or says how proud they are to be your friend, to know you, or be in a relationship with you. It sounds like: *"I'm proud of you," "You have a kind and generous heart,"* and *"I'm so glad I get to be the mom of such an amazing kid!"*

Attention

The need for attention is met when someone calls just to say they were thinking about you or want to spend time with you. It includes our individual undivided attention in effort to get to know people and their needs. The need for attention is also met *when someone attends your event, does the things you like to do or enters your world.* It sounds like: *"Tell me about your day," "How did your test go?" "What would you like to do this weekend?"*

Comfort

The need for comfort is met by *responding to a hurting person with words, feelings, and gentle touch.* There is nothing like the comfort of someone putting an arm around you when you're sad. On other occasions, it is sitting quietly and being present. In the break of unbearable news, it may include crying with you. It sounds like: *"I'm sad for you," "I'm so sorry that you are going through this," "I know you are really disappointed," "I feel compassion for you and what you're going through."*

Encouragement

The need for encouragement involves *cheering for someone who is striving towards a goal.* Encouragement may include a phone call that inspires you on your big day, a note expressing belief in you, or a text that says, *"You can do it!" "Don't give up, keep at it," "I believe in you. You've got this!"*

Respect

The need for respect is met by *treating one another as important and honoring one another with words and actions.* It entails giving a choice to the other person to do something his or her way and listening without interrupting. Respect includes checking with you before making plans that affect you, using an appropriate tone of voice and apologizing when I've done something to hurt you. It sounds like: *"I'd like to hear your ideas," "What do you prefer?" "I was wrong," "Will you forgive me?"*

Security

The need for security is met when a pattern of safety and trust is established. Security is where there are no threats nor aspects of harm for you. Think of what helps you know and feel secure. Think of how it differs from your loved ones. How do they feel secure? You need at least two or more people who assist your needs, do not lose their temper, are dependable and keep thier promise. In the same manner, find ways to fill someone's need for security. It sounds like this: *"I'm here for you. We're going to work this out. I'm going to keep my word to you."*

Support

The need for support is met by coming alongside someone to offer gentle appropriate help with a problem. It includes helping with a big project, teaching someone how to master a skill, or set a strategy to solve an issue. It sounds like: *"I'll be glad to help you. Just let me know. Would you like to try the first step together?"*

See the Need, Fill the Need

Who would the Lord have you bless? A simple move to bless others is to pray with them. Share with them the blessings and challenges you face while giving them a chance to share. Find ways to give first and meet needs. Though it is not always easy to help others with their needs and though the person whose needs are being met shows no gesture of gratefulness, remember you are doing it as unto the Lord. In the process of meeting people's needs, it is the kindness of the Lord that leads people to Himself. You are a reflection of His kindness as He shines through you.

For believers and unbelievers alike, some individuals are instantly impacted by having their needs met, while others need time for God to work in them. When you grow weary, don't give up or give in to lies. Gain strength in prayer, in God's Word, and in the community of saints. When you are refreshed, continue up the path of discipleship by following the Great Commandment and the Great Commission, which includes looking out for the interests of others.

The spiritual path for pilgrims continues to be a tough one, and in some cases, too agonizing to bear, especially for those in the persecuted church. The Christian path is not smooth. Consider counting the cost by asking - Is this path of following Jesus worth it? Jesus promises that His yoke is easy and His burdens are light. Though there are trials, He has overcome the world! The joy, the blessings, the hardships, and the trials do not compare to the prize that will be received in heaven. As if running a race, set your eyes on the finish line. As if on a hike, set your eyes upward.

Upward Discipleship Challenge:

- Read the Kennesaw Mountain Trail Guide on Page 137. Plan a trip to hike up Little Kennesaw and experience Psalm 134.

- Reflect on ways to "bless the Lord" in Psalm 134:1-2. Spend time before the Lord expressing your love to Him.

- Discover your top three relational needs by completing an assessment: **http://bit.ly/2IIY1LV**. Invite the "near ones" in your life to also complete the assessment. Discuss your top needs with one another.

- Look for creative ways to bless one another this week by "giving first."

Continue Upward!

The more we fulfill the Great Commandment, the more we become doers rather than just hearers of God's word. The heights and the depths of God's love change a person. As pilgrims on this earth, our perspective heightens to the truth of who God is, who we are, and who we are meant to be as His creation made in image for His purpose.

The higher one's location is on a mountain, the more the earth's beauty beams from below: the trees, the fields, the towns, the city, the streams, and possibly the array of surrounding mountains and cliffs. In the remote tranquility of nature, the pressures of life grow dim in the granduer of the adventure ahead. In order to take on this journey, the climber had to take the first step. Although you started your spiritual journey, it isn't over yet. It is just the beginning. As we come to the culmination of the Psalms of Ascent, may the Lord bless you as you continue to:

- Turn from deceit to truth (Psalm 120)
- Look by faith only to the Lord (Psalm 121)
- Express gladness to go to the house of the Lord (Psalm 122)
- Find your place of service (Psalm 123)
- Experience the security of the Lord surrounding you (Psalm 124-125)

- Express joy (Psalm 126)
- Walk together as a family (Psalm 127)
- Experience happiness (Psalm 128)
- Press onwards and upwards (Psalm 129)
- Be filled with hope (Psalm 130-131)
- Press on with a long obedience in a same direction (Psalm 132)
- Experience life together in unity (Psalm 133)
- Bless the Lord by ministering to Him (Psalm 134)
- Bless one another by ministering to one another (Psalm 134)

I pray that the study through Psalms of Ascent has given you a form of guidance on your spiritual journey as a disciple of Jesus. As you go forward, I urge you not to rush or dread each step. Enjoy the journey as well as the view– the big picture of what God is doing for you and around you, even in the midst of doubt, confusion, or despair. Realize that you cannot cross over from the depths to God on your own (Ephesians 2:9; Titus 3:5). Realize that God has made a way for you when there is no way (John 14:6). By being broken on the cross for your sin, Jesus has come to your brokenness. Trust in Jesus and find hope! (Romans10:9). Respond to the Lord at the point of His Word. Do today what matters for eternity. Follow Jesus and lead others to follow Jesus with you.

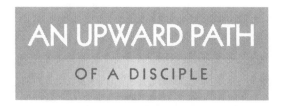

Kennesaw Trail Guide

Jason Schmaltz

Summit Seekers

Experiencing the Psalms of Ascent:

Most people will tell you the reason they hike or run at Kennesaw Mountain is to "escape." Escape from the daily grind or escape from their daily worries or just the noise of life. But what if there was more to life than just trying to "escape" from it? What if instead, you were coming into something when you walked into the woods of this park? A special place. What if God was waiting for you there, in a special spot reserved for you and Him?

Let this book be your guide to that special spot ... and in that special spot, God has just what you need. He has a special place to challenge you, another place to humble you. Other times God wants to show you His awe-inspiring beauty, or give you places to play with your children and delight in their joy. There are many special places where God reveals His blessings to you, and counsels you. You see, God doesn't want you to "escape," He wants you to come be with Him.

As John Muir Says:

"Everybody needs beauty as well as bread, places to play in and pray in, where nature may heal and give strength to body and soul."

Allow this book to help you come play and pray in the presence of God. Observe the healing and Eternal Life given in His presence. Submit to experiencing some of these Psalms in real time. Let's see what happens.

How to use this Guidebook:

There are 8 different modules attached. Each one has directions to a specific part of the park and an activity that you can do there. There are also small maps (ref: caltopo.com) and elevation profiles to show you distances and difficulty. Follow the reading in the modules and that will instruct you how you can actually "experience" the essence of the respective Psalm in real time. There are many different ways and moods in which you can experience these Psalms, so spend some time reading through and decide which experience makes sense for you, then go do it.

Common Map Highlights (ref: caltopo.com):

The overall map shows two main pieces of information. First, are the three key parking areas. You will see in the Psalm modules that these three parking areas are mentioned depending on the area of the park they direct you to. Here you can see them on the map itself. If you want something to type into your GPS that will get you to these parking areas, utilize these addresses:

- **Visitor Center Parking:**
900 Kennesaw Mountain Drive, Kennesaw, GA 30152

- **Burnt Hickory – Old Mountain Road Parking:**
1520 Burnt Hickory Road NW, Marietta

- **Cheatham Hill Parking:** Cheatham Hill Dr SW

The second item shown on the Common Map are the Psalm Labels. This shows about where the area is that you can experience the respective Psalm. Of course, you should review the specific module as it will have a zoomed-in map so you know exactly where to go and what to do. But this Common Map will help you get a good general idea.

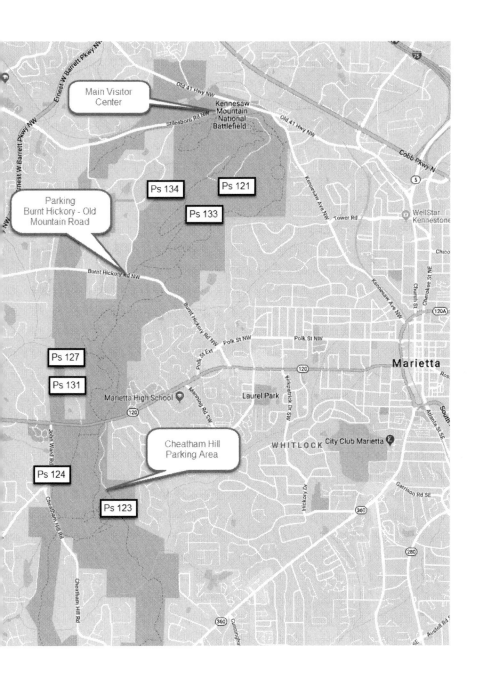

Trail: Boulder areas on Little Kennesaw Trail

Mileage: 3.75 miles out and back

Perfect for: Strength building in groups by climbing the boulders together

Psalm to Experience: Psalm 121

Trail Difficulty: Strenuous – Trail and boulders are some of the more difficult physical challenges in the park

Getting There: Drive to the intersection of Burnt Hickory Road and Old Mountain Road. There is a parking area there that is open from dawn to dusk.

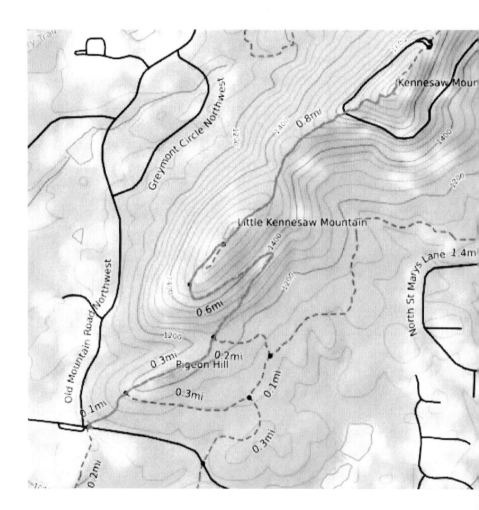

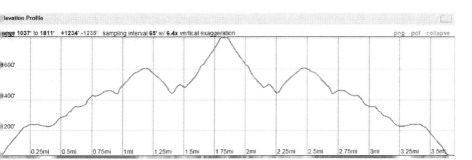

Elevation Profile

range 1037' to 1811'   +1234' -1235'   sampling interval 65' w/ 6.4x vertical exaggeration   png   pdf   collapse

Experiencing Psalm 121:

Activities to Experience:

Climbing the Boulders: There are many large boulder areas on this trail directly, and just off the trail around the saddle between Little Kennesaw Mountain and Big Kennesaw Mountain. Climbing the boulders is one of the most invigorating things you can do in the park. It is also the *most dangerous.*

In rock climbing, it is focus and inner peace that is key to reaching the top of the climb. If you are not focused on exactly what you should be doing, you will lose your footing or miss a hold and the consequences can be severe. Likewise, if you are not at peace but dominated by fear, your muscles will tense up and fatigue quickly. You will not be able to hold on. FOCUS and PEACE. These are the keys. Don't be anxious about what is to come that you may not be able to handle. Don't worry about where your help will come from or how a future problem or anxiety will be solved. God will help you and He will not let you fall (Psalm 121:1-3). Focus on the challenge at hand, focus on the next move to make on the boulder to get to the top. Ask God to help you control the fear. His Holy Spirit is inside whispering, "You got this! I will protect you and keep you safe" (Psalm 121:7).

Take the confidence you felt rock climbing and feel it in your everyday life.

Life Application:

Feel this confidence and the peace in your role as a parent during a challenging time with a child or your role as a spouse. The moves you make to resolve the situation may be difficult, just like the boulder, but God will protect your relationship and make sure you reach the top. At your work, when you are asked to take on a role you think may be overwhelming, God will be there whispering "You got this, I will protect you and keep you safe" (Psalm 121:7). God wants His people to achieve great things, and to help them achieve those things He will protect them through the trials. He never dozes or lets up. He wants to be with you at every moment, overcoming fear and rising to the occasion (Psalm 121:4). All your life, allow God to be your protector in any situation (Psalm 121:8). In this way, you can have the focus and peace to achieve extraordinary feats in your life and He can be glorified.

Safety Note: It is important, if rock climbing outside, that you do so with the correct safety equipment and supervision. If this is not readily available, there is also an excellent indoor rock climbing facility called Stone Summit Kennesaw where you can experience the thrill of rock climbing in a much more controlled environment.

Trail: Illinois Monument Trail

Mileage: 0.25 miles out and back ... you can also do other loop variations through some of the fields mentioned in this book.

Perfect for: Historical perspective and reflection ... you may not want to bring the kids for this one.

Psalm to Experience: Psalm 123

Trail Difficulty: Easy

Getting There: Drive to the Cheatham Hill Parking Area off of Whitlock Avenue at the southern part of the park. Drive all the way back until you cannot go any further and there is a large parking area. From here it is a short hike directly to the monument going south. Otherwise, you can incorporate some of the loops mentioned in other parts of this book.

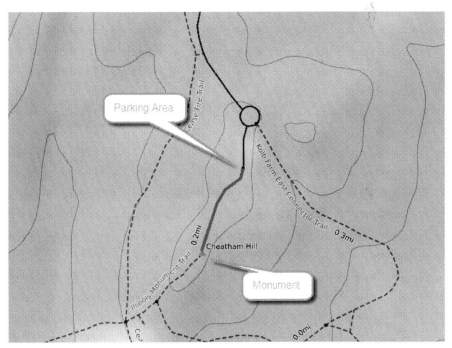

Experiencing Psalm 123:

It is important to remember as you have picnics with your family and fun times in the park, that the reason for the park's preservation was because of a battle of historical significance. The Battle of Kennesaw Mountain was a grueling battle that took place starting June 27, 1864.

June 27 is one of the longest days of the year (Summer Solstice of that year was June 20) and it was also incredibly hot. The location of the Illinois monument is significant in this battle. In the early morning, Union soldiers filtered down in the creek at the base of Cheatham Hill (below the monument). From there, they advanced quietly, and once they reached the Confederate works, they were to signal reinforcements. Unfortunately, as they advanced to within a few yards, the Confederates retaliated with relentless fire power. Both sides dug in and many lives were lost. Multiple officer casualties were felt on the Union side. Both sides fought hard with no relief or support for six days and nights. This specific location was referred to by both sides as the "Dead Angle" due to the amount of casualties felt here.

As you visit the Illinois monument consider the story above. Walk down to the bottom of Cheatham Hill. Now turn and look up and imagine being a young Union Soldier charging the line in the early morning with bullets whizzing past you. Walk up to 100 feet from the monument now. Put yourself in a young soldier's shoes. Imagine being hunkered down, having to make constant effort to minimize your profile lying on your stomach. Try doing it now if you have the strength. Now imagine doing that for six days and nights with NO relief. No breaks, no stretching, no comfort ... and bullets whizzing 12" overhead.

How long in these conditions as a soldier would it be before you looked toward Heaven for some answers? How long until you would be pleading to God to show you some kind of favor? Show us favor, Lord, show us favor, for we've had more than enough contempt (Psalm 123:1-3). As a young soldier, one thing these types of conditions will make you ask yourself is, "Why am I going through this?" Perhaps as you ask that as a Union Soldier in 1864, reflect on your life right now as it is. What battle are you going through right now in which you need God's favor, in which you need God to show up? Like the motivations for the Civil War, how much of your battles are a consequence of arrogance or pride? As God's children, "We've had more than enough scorn from the arrogant and contempt from the proud" (Psalm 123:4). Let God show up in the battle you are fighting right now. Do not dig in indefinitely like the soldiers; this only leads to death. Instead let God come in, let Him walk with you as you take steps to improve your situation. God, please show us favor, our eyes are on You now (Psalm 123:2-3).

Trail: Cease Fire – John Ward Loop

Mileage: 2.5 Mile Loop

Perfect for: Family hikes with small children, picnics, family pictures

Psalm to Experience: Psalm 124

Trail Difficulty: Easy to Moderate – There is one decent hill going up to the Illinois Monument. Other than that, beautiful rolling hills.

Getting There: Drive to the parking area on the southern end of the park on John Ward Road. Park there and then walk across the street to access the loop. Alternatively, you can park at the Cheatham Hill parking area on Whitlock and access the loop from there.

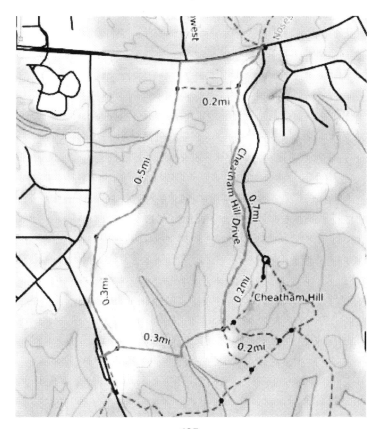

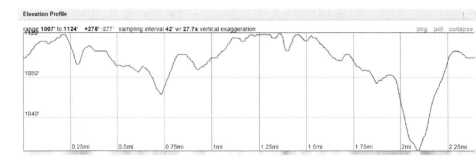

Experiencing Psalm 124:

In this loop you will see many beautiful fields. As you walk through these fields you will experience peace and tranquility as you watch a sea of long grass waving in the sun. Psalm 124:1 says, "What if the Lord had not been on our side?" During the Civil War, these fields were not filled with peace and tranquility, they were filled with anger, hate, and bullets. It was on these fields that our nation nearly self-destructed because too many had put their own interests first instead of the Kingdom of God. As you walk through these fields, imagine opposing soldiers in the brush or in the woods on the boundaries. What type of different emotions and stress would this invoke? "Let us thank the Lord, who has not let our enemies destroy us" (Psalm 124:6), that we as a nation did not swallow ourselves whole (Psalm 124:3). Praise God that the United States was able to overcome the weapons of the enemy: hate, envy, jealousy, and slavery, emerging as a nation that is as peaceful as these fields are now. In the fields, rejoice at the freedom you can experience now. The renewing of life that comes from a spring day stroll on these rolling hills reminds us that, "Our help comes from the Lord, who made heaven and earth" (Psalm 124:8)

Activities to Experience:

Sunrise: One of the best views at the park is these fields during dusk or especially early in the morning at dawn. Nothing can compare to the site of low-level mist just above the grass and the silhouette of a family of deer out for an early morning stroll. Experiencing the sun rise as you walk this loop offers a "live painting" by our Heavenly Creator of the sky and landscape as the light changes. Experience God's handy work 30 minutes before and after sunrise. Special treats are when it is partly cloudy during this time. Set your watch early and get out about 30 minutes before sun rise and let the show begin. "Let us thank the Lord who has not let our enemies destroy us" (Psalm 124:6).

Trail: Noses Creek Trail from Burnt Hickory Rd to Noses Creek
Mileage: 0.7 miles each way
Perfect for: Family hikes with small children, picnics, family pictures
Psalm to Experience: Psalm 127
Train Difficulty: Easy– My two-year-old can hike this trail to the creek and back on her own so don't be afraid to take the young ones. It's not a long way to carry them if they get tired.
Getting There: Drive to the intersection of Burnt Hickory Road and Old Mountain Road. There is a parking area there that's open from dawn to dusk.

Experiencing Psalm 127:

As the Psalm says, "It is vain for you to rise up early, to sit up late, to eat the bread of sorrows ... Behold, children are a heritage from the Lord, the fruit of the womb is a reward."

As a father or mother, we can easily become caught up in our tasks and obligations. Noses Creek Trail allows an opportunity to leave those obligations in the parking lot to be dealt with later and focus on the reward the Lord has given us in the form of our children. This trail is great, especially for small children, to start stretching their legs and experiencing the outdoors as God intended. It is best if mom and dad are there to walk side by side with them and watch as they explore the limitless boundaries of God's wilderness. Put the phones in "airplane mode" and enjoy watching your children explore and realize new things about their abilities and strength. You want to be fully attentive when your child turns to you to show you how muddy they got in the creek or what stick they found or how fast they were able to run up to the infantry monument.

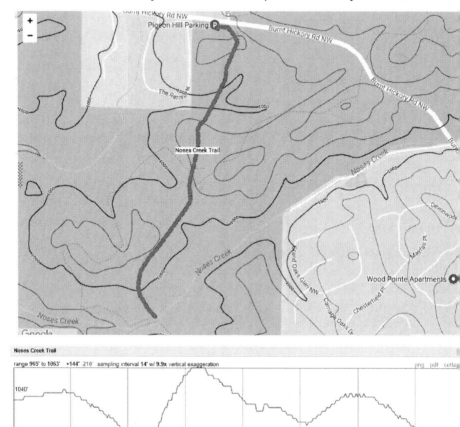

Two activities for the whole family to experience:

Picnic at the creek: Hike down to Noses Creek with a late lunch or early dinner packed and enjoy an afternoon or evening with the family. The simple act of playing in a creek for a child is something sacred and special for all children. This should be enjoyed by both the children and the parents. Don't have a backend appointment ... let the kids get in their experience. Then, when it's time for the meal, share a devotional with your family. What a great time to explain to your kids that God has provided this cathedral to you so that He could be a part of your household (Psalm 127:1).

Pictures at the Battle Field: Arrive at the parking area in late evening just as the sun has about 1-2 hours left. From the trail heading south from the parking lot, you can get a lot of great pictures in the shade of the large trees. This will offer you a chance to control the light with the shade and also have an amazing backdrop with the old trees. Have a picnic there, taking pictures constantly as the sun goes down to capture the different lighting effects. Additionally, at the top of the other field on the right, you should try to grab a picture of the kids playing in the field just as the sun is setting over the horizon. If you have cute kids, which I'm sure you do, this natural lighting will provide a Divine Photo Studio to capture the essence of your child's spirit and also that of your family. What a joy to be able to celebrate God's blessing of the next generation of the Body of Christ. "Happy is a man who has his quiver full of them" (Psalm 127:5). Indeed.

Trail: All trails during Autumn

Mileage: NA

Perfect for: Reflection and Thanksgiving for God's Blessings on you and your family

Psalm to Experience: Psalm 128

Trail Difficulty: Varying depending on which trail you choose

Getting There: Experiencing Psalm 128 can be done at any of the trails, the key will be going between Late October and mid-November. This is the peak of fall foliage and this is God's blessing to experience in this Psalm. The best week is the first week in November typically.

Experiencing Psalm 128:

All year long we work hard to provide for our family and make ends meet. At times it is difficult to realize how truly blessed we are as we get caught up with the daily struggles of work, family logistics, and keeping up our affairs. In the South, God has blessed us with an opportunity to break away from the daily routine during the Fall as His presence and beauty is revealed to us through the changing of the season. Just as we start to enter the season of Thanksgiving, God will provide a break from the summer heat with cool dry air and the most beautiful display of colors as the fall foliage commences. What an opportunity to enjoy this with your family and realize how much God has blessed you in this time of Thanksgiving.

During the peak of Fall foliage, take your family out for a walk in this live painting that God wants you to be a part of. As you prepare a picnic or snack with your spouse and children, reflect on Psalm 128:1-2: "How happy is everyone who fears the Lord, who walks in his ways! You will surely eat what your hands have worked for. You will be happy and it will go well for you." In God's masterpiece that stimulates all five senses, enjoy a meal together with the ones you love.

Now it is time to give thanks for God's blessings. It is good to do this with your spouse and kids if they are old enough to participate. Share words of affirmation with each other. Be thankful to God for a husband who fears the Lord and is blessed because he brings God into the family church daily. Thank God for his strength and that God is present in his heart and mind as he protects and guides our family (Psalm 128:4). How blessed a man is to have a wife who provides love and nourishment to a household! It is God working through her strength and finesse that over time transforms four walls and a roof into a home. Thank you God for my wife who does this effortlessly (Psalm 128:3). What a joy it is to be part of the living water as it flows from the Holy Spirit through the parents and trickles into the children as they grow like young olive trees around your table (Psalm 128:3).

Pray with your family now as your meal concludes. As you see the leaves changing and falling, don't forget to look at the tree roots themselves. At first glance, they may appear to not be changing at all, but as a tree grows up, the roots grow deep and become more and more firm. Likewise pray to God that as your family grows up, that your Godly roots grow deep. Pray that the Lord continues to bless your family so you will see prosperity for all the days of your life and will see your children's children! Peace be with you and your family (Psalm 128:5-6).

Trail: Noses Creek Trail – Hardage Mill Loop

Mileage: 3.4 miles total

Perfect for: Solitude, reflection, quite time.

Psalm to Experience: Psalm 131

Trail Difficulty: Moderate with some strenuous parts. There is one sustained climb if you go south on Noses Creek Trail and then on Hardage Mill Trail there are some short but intense climbs. Plenty of nice places for a break though.

Getting There: Drive to the intersection of Burnt Hickory Road and Old Mountain Road. There is a parking area there open from dawn to dusk.

Experiencing Psalm 131:

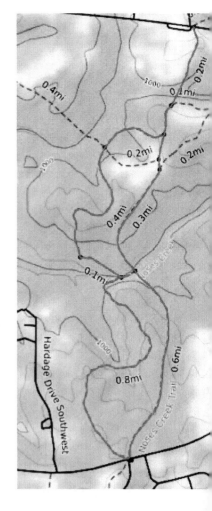

Many times, we find ourselves fighting to protect our identity and ego as we navigate career choices, family dynamics, and daily stressors in a "keep up with the Jones's" society. As you enter into this quiet loop, experience the pressures of work and society lift off your shoulders. Rejoice as "Instead [you] are content and at peace. As a child lies quietly in its mother's arms, so [your] heart is quiet within [you]" (Psalm 131:2). Sit by the creek and experience God's soothing whisper of water trickling over the rocks as he tries to soothe your racing mind and thoughts. Submit to the soothing whisper. Experience the shelter of the canopy that will protect you from the worries. No matter what your situation was when you entered the forest, surrender it to your Father as he soothes you. Spend some time

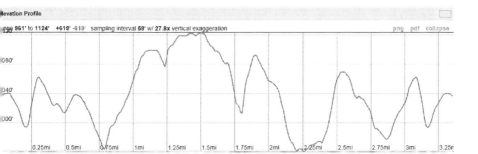

in meditation by the water. Talk to God as the sun sets over the big field on the north end of this loop. "Trust in the Lord now and forever!" (Ps 131:3) and emerge out of the forest with a humble trust in your Heavenly Father.

Activity to Experience:

Prayer time by the creek: There is a small side creek on the southern end of Hardage Mill Trail between the main creek and Whitlock. This is a very well-kept secret spot where you can have quiet time with God as you recharge after the big ascent you just did going south on Noses Creek. Pray like this:

- Become fully present. "Give up your pride ... you're not concerned with great matters or difficult subjects" (Ps. 131:1).

- Remove your ego. "Turn away from your arrogance" (Ps. 131:1). You don't have to be on guard here.
- Engage in prayer now ... take your time ... you don't have to hurry.
- Take some breaths ... ask God to come into this place: "God come visit with me."
- Take some more breaths ... listen to His soothing voice through the trickle of the creek.
- Take some more breaths ... feel His warmth ... feel the peace.
- Sometimes in prayer you don't have to ask for anything, or thank God for anything ... sometimes, you get to just feel His presence. This is a good place for that.
- "God I trust in you now and forever" (Ps. 131:3).

Trail: Little Kennesaw

Mileage: 1 to 3 miles out and back

Perfect for: Intimate group discussions

Psalm to Experience: Psalm 133

Trail Difficulty: Moderate to Strenuous – Trail is steep in parts but overall not very long to the meeting areas

Getting There: Drive to the intersection of Burnt Hickory Road and Old Mountain Road. There is a parking area there open from dawn to dusk. There are two good spots for intimate group meetings slightly off trail.

First intimate meeting spot: At the first main switchback as you are ascending Little Kennesaw Mountain, instead of following the trail at the switchback, veer off north and scramble off trail for about 30 yards. You will see a large rock clearing that allows for multiple people to visit and have discussion. This area is exposed and good for sunrises or sunsets but not so good on hot days at high noon.

Second intimate meeting spot: At the saddle between Little Kennesaw Mountain and Kennesaw Mountain, veer off trail west toward some boulders after the little hump between the two mountains. As you are walking off trail, you will see a clearing that can provide an excellent intimate spot for having a group discussion. It is far enough off trail that nobody will notice you but close enough that you can still see the trail. This area is shaded so it is better for warmer days as you will get some nice relief and usually a breeze going over the saddle of the mountain.

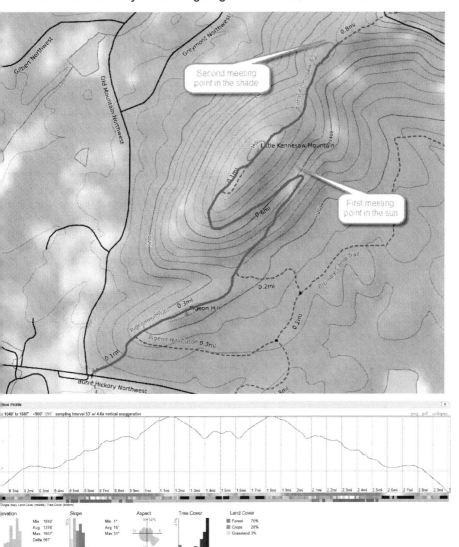

Experiencing Psalm 133:

These days every man and woman seems to be in their own personal silo. With social media, mobile devices, and email, it is rare to have a social interaction with a person who is directly in front of you anymore, let alone a group discussion. The simple intimacy that eye contact offers has been lost in most of our day to day communication. Let's change the rules with Psalm 133 and round up a couple of our brothers or sisters, pack some tea or water, and head up the mountain for some *real* facetime!

Enjoy the brief workout that you are going to get as you climb the back of Little Kennesaw Mountain from the parking lot. Catching up on life's on-goings with one another during this time is a perfect way to refamiliarize yourself with your group. As you approach one of the meeting spots mentioned above, enjoy picking out the best seat for you that enables you to see all the group members and have a nice view of God's creation. Perhaps at this point you want to bless the intimate conversation with an opening prayer, or maybe you just want to verbalize how happy you are to have your close friends all in one place with no distractions. Be sure to turn off your phones ... you won't need them for this group chat.

As you pull out your water bottles or start to make some tea, it's time to move past the pleasantries you were sharing before and share what's really on your mind with the people you care about. Perhaps you have a devotional to share with your friends. Share how it relates to your life. Or maybe you have a developing situation in your life and you wish to now get some advice from your friends. Maybe you have nothing planned to discuss, in which case, to move into a meaningful conversation, consider going around your circle and sharing either a big struggle or big victory that each of you is experiencing in life right now. As intimate details are shared, be careful not to judge, but instead to embrace the intimacy of brotherhood or sisterhood as the intimacy brings your group closer. Build one another up and offer up ideas to help one another. Let the walls down. Give in to vulnerability through tears of joy or tears of sorrow; you don't need to be on guard here. "How good and pleasant it is when brothers (or sisters) live together in harmony" (Psalm 133:1).

How wonderful are the friendships that God has placed in your life! As you begin to close your conversation, provide words of affirmation to one another. Tell each other what the years or decades of friendship have meant to you. During this experience, have you felt God working through you? Have you experienced Him blessing the conversations and individual relationships as a whole? Not just as a group of single relationships, but as a Brotherhood or Sisterhood? What a blessing it is to feel God's presence "like the dew of Mt. Hermon falling on the mountains of Zion. For there the Lord has appointed the blessing – life forevermore" (Psalm 133:3).

Trail: Little Kennesaw
Mileage: 2.2 miles out and back
Perfect for: Evening worship service at sunset with God and loved ones
Psalm to Experience: Psalm 134
Trail Difficulty: Moderate to Strenuous – Trail is steep in parts but overall not very long
Getting There: Drive to the intersection of Burnt Hickory Road and Old Mountain Road. There is a parking area there open from dawn to dusk.
Tip: *Bring a headlamp so you can stay for the whole sunset and then use your headlamp to get back to your car. The park service will not lock your car in the parking area.*

Experiencing Psalm 134:

You will want to make special plans to attend this evening worship service at the park. Park the car about an hour before sunset and pack some tea, a loaf of bread, a pocket Bible and head up the back side of the mountain to find a special cathedral just before the top of Little Kennesaw (right before you get to the canyons). There are some bluffs just off the trail facing southwest and this is where God has reserved seating for you and your loved ones. As the sun begins to descend open your pocket Bible and share your favorite Psalm of Ascent with the other members of the worship service. Bless the Lord with all those present as you share God's Message at His worship service (Psalm 134:1).

Welcome in the Lord's presence as your young children climb on each rock to get the best seat as the worship service commences with pink hues and orange outlines of clouds. God has blessed you with special unique

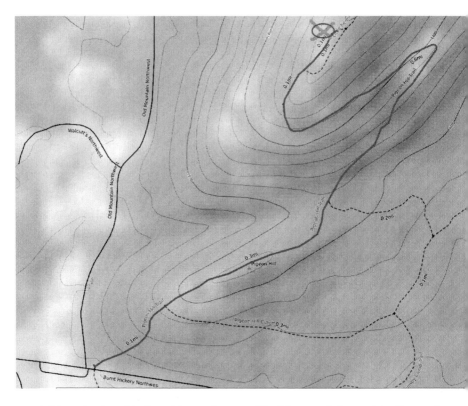

children just as He has blessed you with this special worship through a unique sunset. No need to snap pictures or have your mind anywhere else but here. As your children continue to play in God's warmth, start to visit with God through prayer and meditation. No distractions up here, commit all your attention to visiting with God. "Lift up your hands in the holy place and bless the Lord" (Psalm 134:2).

The sunset comes to a climax as it crosses the horizon and the painting develops rapidly. Enjoy being immersed in God's beauty as He displays true mastery of His creation. As the sun is eclipsed, the clouds change colors rapidly from orange to pink to purple and ultimately the stencil masterpiece transitions into evening. The painting has come and gone. However, the Lord has worked his master craftsmanship into you as well. Your traits, your strengths, your passions, your heart are all crafted by Him and are as beautiful as the sunset you just witnessed ... but He wants you to live forever. Jesus has come to give you eternal life so that you live in true peace as His creation (John 5:24). What a blessing! This is the thought you take back as you descend off the mountain. "May the Lord, Maker of heaven and earth (and incredible sunsets), bless you from Zion" (Psalm 134:3).

ABOUT THE AUTHOR

Jason Schmaltz

I was originally born in Roanoke, Virginia and spent my early childhood living in the Appalachian Foothills, climbing trees, fishing in creeks, and rolling in the occasional patch of poison ivy. Our family then moved to the metro Atlanta area, where I went to high school in Cobb County and then went to Georgia Tech to major in Chemical Engineering.

I moved to Louisiana to pursue my career, and there I met my wife Anna, who was a ballet dancer and invited me to see her dance the Arabian in the Nutcracker. We moved from Baton Rouge to Houston to start our new life together. My childhood tree climbing days were all but a distant memory in the concrete jungle of Houston until I embarked on a hiking trip in New Mexico. Climbing through the Sandia Mountains, I reconnected with my passion for the outdoors. It was undeniable that the outdoors would have to be a regular part of my life.

Shortly after that trip, I quit my job in Houston and my wife and I moved just north of Atlanta to start a family and be within striking distance of the Great Smoky Mountains. We now have three great kids, Johnny (5), Naomi (3), and Heidi (newborn). When I'm not chasing them around, you can find me running up some mountain somewhere with the same spirit of a young boy seeing the world for the first time.

I've traveled the world but have never found a place as beautiful and diverse as America, both in culture and landscape. There is a special discipleship group I lead for men called the **Summit Seekers Experience.**

Summit Seekers Experience

The Summit Seekers Experience allows a man to fully realize his strengths and passions by utilizing them to accomplish God's purpose for his life.

There is a special kind of life that Jesus talks about in John 5 and John 10 called the Eternal Life. Although this refers to our life after we die, this is also a life we can have right NOW. Jesus tells us that he has come for us to live life in all it's fullness, to live life to the limit (John 10:10). **Summit Seekers Experience** is a program that helps to facilitate men to arrive to that point. Imagine living every day with a divine confidence that you are going to fulfill your purpose. Imagine living that everyday and doing it with others. Does it sound possible? It is possible, and this is what God wants for you.

Check out the **Summit Seekers Experience** *website:*

www.summitseekersexperience.org

Prepare yourself for the ultimate transformational journey.

APPENDIX

End notes

CHAPTER 1

1   Eugene H. Peterson, A Long Obedience in the Same Direction: Discipleship in an Instant Society, (Kindle Edition, IVP Books), 1812-1814.

CHAPTER 2

2   https://hackemoon.com/how-much-time-do-people-spend-on-their-mobile-phones-in-2017-e5f90a0b10a6

CHAPTER 4

3   E. Lewellen, D. Mangum, D. R. Brown, R. Klippenstein, & R. Hurst, Eds., Servant, Lexham Theological Wordbook. (Bellingham, WA: Lexham Press, 2014).

4   Peterson, 739-741.

5   R. Jamieson, A. R. Fausset, & D. Brown, Commentary Critical and Explanatory on the Whole Bible, Vol. 1, (Oak Harbor, WA: Logos Research Systems, Inc.,1997), 385.

CHAPTER 6

6   R. G. Bratcher, & W. D. Reyburn, A Translator's Handbook on the Book of Psalms, (New York: United Bible Societies,1991), 1072.

CHAPTER 7

7   J. D. Barry, D. Mangum, D. R. Brown, M. S. Heiser, M. Custis, E. Ritzema, ... D. Bomar, (2012, 2016). Faithlife Study Bible (Psalm 128:1), (Bellingham, WA: Lexham Press).

8   http://www.azquotes.com/quote/578784

9   Peterson, 1559-1561.

10 M. Custis, Fearing God in the Old Testament, Faithlife Study Bible, (Bellingham, WA: Lexham Press, 2012, 2016).

11 Bratcher & Reyburn, 1076.

12 Bratcher & Reyburn, 1077.

13 https://www.citylab.com/transportation/2015/04/global-car-motorcycle-and-bike-ownership-in-1-infographic/390777/

14 J. D. Barry et.al., Psalm 128:5, Faithlife Study Bible.

CHAPTER 8

15 Peterson, 1559-1561.

16 R. Jamieson, et. al., Vol. 1, 386.

17 Peterson, 1645-1647.

CHAPTER 9

18 ©Salvador Dalí Museum, Inc. St. Petersburg, FL 2017.

19 R. Jamieson, et. al., Vol. 1, 386.

20 Peterson, 1812-1814.

21 Peterson.

22 Peterson.

23 Bratcher & Reyburn, 1085.

24 J. D. Barry et.al., Psalm 130:8, Faithlife Study Bible.

25 Bratcher & Reyburn, 1085.

CHAPTER 10

26 M. H. Woudstra, Ark of the Covenant, Baker Encyclopedia of the Bible, Vol. 1, (Grand Rapids, MI: Baker Book House, 1988), 170.

27 R. Jamieson, et. al., Vol. 1, 386.

28 J. D. Barry et.al., Psalm 130:8, Faithlife Study Bible.

29 R. Jamieson, et. al., Vol. 1, 386.

30 I Samuel 1:11, Peterson, Eugene H., The Message

CHAPTER 11

31 Bratcher & Reyburn, 1096.

32 A. P. Ross, Psalms, The Bible Knowledge Commentary: An Exposition of the Scriptures, Vol. 1, J. F. Walvoord and R. B. Zuck, Eds., (Wheaton, IL: Victor Books, 1985), 888.

33 Peterson.

34 Bratcher & Reyburn, 1097.

35 Peterson, 2260-2262.

36 J. D. Barry et.al., Psalm 133:3, Faithlife Study Bible.

37 Peterson.

38 Ross, 888.

39 Bratcher & Reyburn, 1098.

CHAPTER 12

40 Desiring the Kingdom, Worship, Worldview, and Cultural Formation, Vol. 1, 56.

41 Impact Study Bible, Following Jesus.